T0274950

Carthage

ARCHAEOLOGICAL HISTORIES

Series editors: Thomas Harrison, Duncan Garrow and Michele George

An important series charting the history of sites, buildings and towns from their construction to the present day. Each title examines not only the physical history and uses of the site but also its broader context: its role in political history, in the history of scholarship, and in the popular imagination.

Carthage

*Sandra Bingham and
Eve MacDonald*

BLOOMSBURY ACADEMIC
LONDON • NEW YORK • OXFORD • NEW DELHI • SYDNEY

BLOOMSBURY ACADEMIC
Bloomsbury Publishing Plc
50 Bedford Square, London, WC1B 3DP, UK
1385 Broadway, New York, NY 10018, USA
29 Earlsfort Terrace, Dublin 2, Ireland

BLOOMSBURY, BLOOMSBURY ACADEMIC and the Diana logo are trademarks of
Bloomsbury Publishing Plc

First published in Great Britain 2024

Copyright © Sandra Bingham and Eve MacDonald, 2024

Sandra Bingham and Eve MacDonald have asserted their right under the Copyright,
Designs and Patents Act, 1988, to be identified as Authors of this work.

For legal purposes the Acknowledgements on p. ix constitute an
extension of this copyright page.

Cover design: Terry Woodley
Cover image © Westend61/Getty

All rights reserved. No part of this publication may be reproduced or transmitted in
any form or by any means, electronic or mechanical, including photocopying,
recording, or any information storage or retrieval system, without prior
permission in writing from the publishers.

Bloomsbury Publishing Plc does not have any control over, or responsibility for,
any third-party websites referred to or in this book. All internet addresses given
in this book were correct at the time of going to press. The author and publisher regret
any inconvenience caused if addresses have changed or sites have ceased to exist,
but can accept no responsibility for any such changes.

A catalogue record for this book is available from the British Library.

Library of Congress Cataloging-in-Publication Data
Names: Bingham, Sandra, author. | MacDonald, Eve, author.
Title: Carthage / Sandra Bingham and Eve MacDonald.
Description: New York : Bloomsbury Academic, 2024. | Series: Archaeological histories |
Includes bibliographical references and index.
Identifiers: LCCN 2023054456 (print) | LCCN 2023054457 (ebook) |
ISBN 9781472522764 (paperback) | ISBN 9781472529299 (hardback) |
ISBN 9781472528902 (pdf) | ISBN 9781472526946 (ebook)
Subjects: LCSH: Excavations (Archaeology)–Tunisia–Carthage (Extinct city) |
Museums–Acquisitions–Europe, Western–History. |
Carthage (Extinct city–History–To 1500. | Carthage (Extinct city)–Antiquities.
Classification: LCC DT269.C33 (print) | LCC DT269.C33 (ebook) |
DDC 939./73—dc23/eng/20240131
LC record available at https://lccn.loc.gov/2023054456
LC ebook record available at https://lccn.loc.gov/2023054457

ISBN: HB: 978-1-4725-2929-9
       PB: 978-1-4725-2276-4
       ePDF: 978-1-4725-2890-2
       eBook: 978-1-4725-2694-6

Series: Archaeological Histories

Typeset by RefineCatch Limited, Bungay, Suffolk
Printed and bound in Great Britain

To find out more about our authors and books visit www.bloomsbury.com
and sign up for our newsletters.

CONTENTS

ILLUSTRATIONS

MAPS AND PLANS

ACKNOWLEDGEMENTS

This book has been a long time in gestation. When we first began thinking about it almost twenty years ago, the now ex-President Zine al-Abidine Ben Ali was well entrenched in Tunisia and there was no expectation that things would change anytime soon. But over the past two decades, much has changed. From the Arab Spring to the current political shifts in Tunisia, the country has transformed over twenty years, as have the views towards archaeology, politics, history and heritage, and the ways these influence our understanding of ancient sites. There have also been big shifts in the study of archaeology and the technologies available to those working in the field. As a result, we believe that this is a much better book. The publication of Prof. Abdelmajid Ennabli's award-winning volume on Carthage in 2020 was also a great help to us in checking our facts. His knowledge of the site and its history is unparalleled.

There are far too many people to acknowledge who have helped on this long road. A special mention must be made of those who kept encouraging us not to forget Carthage and who have been generous with their time and conversation, in particular, colleagues at the University of Edinburgh, Ulrike Roth and Lucy Grig, and at Cardiff University. But the greatest support came from those who joined us for our writers' retreats in the Highlands of Scotland. Thanks to Stephen Copp and Keith Tracey for the fine wine and good conversation.

Introduction

To visit Carthage today is to see a famous site, a city of legend, of curses, of martyrdoms and conquests, and yet what is immediately clear is that these ancient legacies are not easily accessed in the landscape. There is a kind of hidden nature to the place and its archaeology. The site does not present itself outright, as equally famous ancient cities like Athens or Rome, but is preserved in bits and pieces across a landscape of great natural beauty on the north coast of Africa in the modern country of Tunisia. This stunning location was part of the reason the place was coveted by so many different peoples over the thousands of years of its existence. That the ancient remains do not stand out by themselves, and the reasons for this, are the purpose of this book. This is the story of how the city of Carthage was inhabited, abandoned, imagined and created in the period after it stopped being an ancient city, and what impact that had on the archaeology and its interpretations.

An archaeological site is made up of many things. It is never simply a matter of what is there on or in the ground. It is also necessary to factor into the story who did the excavating and what their motivation was. The prevailing winds of interpretation have changed dramatically since the beginnings of archaeological investigation and brought different perspectives to the fore at different periods of history. Things have changed over the period we have been writing this book, much less over the past thousand years or so. From its vantage point in the middle of the Mediterranean, there are very few perspectives that have not influenced how we understand Carthage as a place alongside its archaeological heritage. Interpreting this heritage and understanding the site will always be influenced by those who control access to it and their views of the relevance of the place. How Carthage and its heritage served the people in charge of the bigger picture (whether an empire, kingdom, state or nation) over the many years of its post-ancient existence has influenced how we understand the ancient city. Archaeology, politics and history are endlessly intertwined and a place like Carthage is a perfect example of this.

The very name Carthage still evokes images and layers of a past both magnificent and traumatic. As a place, as a contested space, a city, a ruin, it is one of the most intriguing in all history. There are so many different narratives of ancient Carthage to contend with, voices and stories told by all of those who came and settled and built and conquered and destroyed and then observed and studied there. From the foundation by colonial settlers from the Phoenician city of Tyre to conquest by Rome, to the rise of the Arab kingdom of Tunis and the French colonial occupation, it is a site of memory and history like few others. This is the story of the place in all these many guises and from many different narratives. This book focuses on the way the space that Carthage occupied in the landscape was built up, taken down, reused, left to ruin and then excavated and developed and reimagined as a twentieth-century suburb of Tunis. The work of archaeology at Carthage in the twenty-first century continues in pace with the thriving neighbourhood of Tunis that inhabits it today. These two aspects exist side by side and not always in an easy neighbourly way.

It is a complicated process to study and write about Carthage and here we have approached the task through the place itself as well as through the key actors and actions that had an impact on the way the site was preserved. This in turn has been instrumental in the way the history of Carthage is remembered. There are two aspects of Carthage that weave back and forth throughout this story. The legends and memories of the ancient city and culture, contrasted with the realities on the ground – a kind of symbiotic relationship between the idea of the place and the practicalities found there. These two aspects are at play throughout the period of the post-ancient occupation of Carthage and combine the intellectual curiosity about a famous ancient city with the evolving study of archaeology and the interpretations of remains and discoveries that have filled our knowledge. These guide our story.

The story of Carthage is also the story of the Mediterranean and how the coastal regions of North Africa fit into that history. We have attempted to include the context of key events in Mediterranean history that affected the site and connect these to moments where the study of the ancient city advanced or was influenced from beyond the limits of its territory. There are both macro and micro histories at work in the creation of archaeological sites and the first two chapters of this book look at the story of the ancient and medieval and early modern Mediterranean and the role that Carthage and then Tunis played. Macro historical events and figures set the narrative of the city, but in many ways it is the micro history that has created the state of the archaeological site itself. There is then a strain of the book that focuses on engagement with the local landscape over thousands of years in parallel to the macro history. Medieval Arab scholars, many from the regions of North Africa, who travelled across the vast world of Dar el-Islam, began to place their cities and culture into the wider history of a new world. The beginning of European antiquarian enquiry and formal archaeological research at Carthage began in the late eighteenth and nineteenth centuries as the discipline itself developed. As in many parts of the world, this coincided with the advent of European colonial interest in North Africa. There was then a dissonance created through some of these processes between the populations who lived on the ground and around the site and those who studied and were interested in the ruins and finds. This colonial overlay is the lens through which much of the history is still viewed today, and while this is being deconstructed as we write, there is still a profound influence.

The book covers a long period of time, from the early foundations of the Phoenician city in the ninth century BCE to the current issues of archaeological preservation and development at Carthage in the twenty-first century. This inevitably means we have engaged in forms of breaking down the periods into entities that are both well-known and sometimes less evident. It also means that the work is not comprehensive and that there are omissions – in particular, people and periods only briefly mentioned. We have tried to focus on pivotal moments in the creation of the archaeological site and also in the public and wider perceptions of Carthage.

The city foundations we have dated from the most up-to-date research and C14 data, which places occupation at the site in the latter part of the ninth century BCE. This corresponds with the ancient literary sources that claim the date to be in this range as well. There has been an explosion of archaeological research on the Phoenician Mediterranean over the past two decades that has begun to reshape our understanding of Carthage as an early Iron Age site in the Mediterranean. Throughout the book we use terminology that reflects conventional use. So, the word Phoenician is used to refer to the cultures of the Mediterranean that thrived from early in the first millennium BCE and originated in the region of the Levant now known as Lebanon, Israel and Palestine. The city of Carthage was founded by people from the city state of Tyre, according to legend, who spoke the Phoenician language. The word Punic refers to the city and culture of Carthage as a colonial descendent of Tyre, both similar and yet distinct from Phoenician because of the rise of Carthage as its own powerful entity in the western Mediterranean from the period of the sixth to fifth centuries until the second century BCE. The city of Roman Carthage was an imperial provincial capital and evolved into a late antique city with a strong Christian identity which then became the capital of the Vandal kingdom of North Africa, only to be conquered and occupied by the eastern Roman Empire in the sixth century CE. We use the term 'Byzantine' for this period because it is conventional to refer to the world of the Roman Emperor Justinian as the Byzantine Empire, while we acknowledge that it is inaccurate and a post-ancient construct.

The Arab–Muslim conquest of North Africa in the late seventh century creates a whole new range of terminologies and identities, including the ninth-century Aghlabids who began as Abbasid governors and ruled the central Mediterranean zone for a century. The succeeding Fatimid period lasted from the tenth to twelfth century and was succeeded by the Almohads. The Hafsid kingdom of Tunis arose from the autochthonous people of the region (while claiming descent from the Rashidun Caliph Omar) in the thirteenth century. The Hafsids reflect an indigenous identity and underlying narrative of the people who lived in the region throughout this whole period and who have continued to be the majority ethnic population. Words like Libyan, Numidian and Moor all reflect ancient names for the autochthonous (often now referred to as Amazigh) people, and we employ these terms when they are used in a specific context or quotation or reference to ancient material. The term Berber is also frequently used in the scholarship and sources and refers to the indigenous peoples of North Africa who lived there before the coming of Islam.[1]

With the demise of the Hafsids in the sixteenth century, the Ottoman period saw the establishment of the eyalet of Tunis (*Eyālet-i Tunus* in Turkish), a provincial-type status. This then evolved into the period of the Beylik (1705–1881), which was a more autonomous rule in Tunis and Carthage under the Husaynid dynasty. The beys who ruled were still, nonetheless, under the auspices of the Ottoman sultan. The French Protectorate was officially established in 1883 and lasted through to Tunisian independence in 1956. We have tried to be consistent in the use of the terminology to reflect these specific periods and their impact on the archaeology of the site of Carthage. This early modern world was the key moment between observational interactions at Carthage to more specific and scientific investigations of the ancient remains at the site.

How does this book work? Many archaeologists, scholars and historians have come before us here and their work has allowed this book to be written. There are many conventions and issues about sources and material that we have tried to deal with consistently and with the most up-to-date research in mind. The endnotes serve as a bibliography of key texts while other essential reading has been included in a general bibliography. This is by no means exhaustive but serves to provide a resource for those who might want to delve deeper into the many issues and histories presented.

Like the city itself, the scholarship on ancient Carthage is not uniform or unilingual. This is a book written for a wide audience and intended to be accessible for non-specialists. We have decided, for example, to use non-diacritic anglicized Arabic names for ease of reading in English and have tried to be consistent in the transliteration. We have used the titles of works accessed in English or French generally (with any other versions supplied in the bibliography). We have used our own translations where possible but where better translations exist, we have used those, and they are also cited in the endnotes. It is important to acknowledge that much of the scholarship on ancient Carthage has not been written in English, and that Arabic, French, German, Dutch, Italian and Spanish language scholarship has been hugely important and useful here. We have included the key publications and also note that their full bibliographies can take readers further in depth into the various subject matters.

This book is about a place on the southern shores of the Mediterranean, right in the middle of the sea, and the people who interacted with it over millennia and how this created the archaeological site of Carthage we see today. It is also about the way that archaeology and its intentions have shifted our understanding of that site and transformed it over the past two centuries. It is far from a simple story as the multiple layers of history, identity and occupation of the place itself reflect. There is not one Carthage but hundreds of them and each version might hold a different meaning for the observer. Here we have tried to tie together some key themes to help those interested in learning more about Carthage as a place and those who might want to visit it and get a sense of the lay of the land. We hope it is a story of the importance of understanding the past and how that is shaped by the intentions of those who study it and how there are few, if any, absolutes when it comes to the interpretations of history.

1

From Carthage to Rome

A Brief Overview

Tales of ancient Carthage have always fuelled the imagination. The epic and tragic telling of Carthaginian history – by others inevitably – and the reception of the city have deeply influenced our understanding of the archaeological remains at the site. Old Carthage was a city of myth and legendary wealth in Roman times and evoked passionate and engaging debate. The Romans who destroyed the first incarnation of Carthage reoccupied the site with their citizens and, on the ruins of the old, built a new city that would become one of the largest and most prosperous in the Roman Empire. Carthage then had many lives in the ancient world, and its history is of many ages: Iron Age foundations in the ninth century BCE, growth in the Archaic period through to the Hellenistic, Roman, Vandal and Byzantine occupations, continuing to the very limits of antiquity in the seventh century CE. The archaeological site of Carthage reflects this long history and through its remains we can glimpse the way the site was used, reused, built, torn down, adapted, buried, destroyed and remembered over the 1,500 years of its occupation.

In a Mediterranean-focused world, Carthage occupied the geographically perfect location (see Map 1.1). Situated on the north coast of the African continent, where the sea narrows between the island of Sicily and the region of North Africa, Carthage commanded the sailing route from east to west and back. Sitting on the wide Gulf of Tunis provided natural protection for ships during bad weather and the siting of Carthage at the innermost point of the gulf meant that the city was protected on all sides by water if attacked by land (Polybius 1.73.3–6). The hinterland of Carthage was extremely fertile and agriculturally rich. As a result, Carthage became a prosperous and multicultural city soon after its first foundation by citizens from Tyre (in present-day Lebanon) in the ninth century BCE. It was called *Qart Hadasht* (the New City) in the Phoenician tongue and this name is Graeco-Romanized to Carthage. This first city developed over time and combined Tyrian,

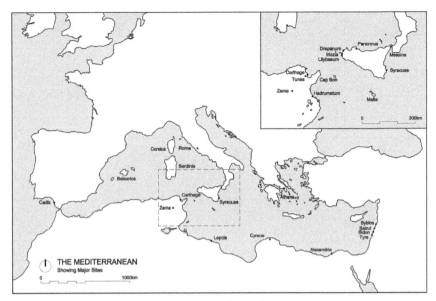

MAP 1.1 *Carthage in the Mediterranean (drawn by Stephen Copp).*

indigenous North African and multi-Mediterranean cultures. It would be a
dominant presence in the central and western Mediterranean until its
destruction by the Romans in 146 BCE.

In legend and stories, the foundation by Tyrians was never forgotten and
a strong connection was maintained between the two cities throughout the
first incarnation of Carthage. According to two of our ancient sources, a
tithe from Carthage was delivered to the treasury of the Great Temple of
Melqart at Tyre on an annual basis (Polybius 31.4.12; Diodorus Siculus
20.14.1–2). Melqart, the Tyrian god syncretized in antiquity with the Greek
hero Herakles, was one of the founding deities of Carthage. The god played
an integral role in supporting and sustaining new Phoenician settlements
across the Mediterranean. This is in much the same way as Herakles did for
the early Greek settlements in the western Mediterranean. In fact, some
inscriptions at Carthage carry the identifier 'sons of Tyre', which scholars
argue could be linked to tracing family origins back to the first colonists
from that city and the patron deity.[1] Tyrian heritage was a strong and proud
part of the many different components that made up the Carthaginian
people. Roman memories of ancient Carthage also preserved this link
and Virgil's epic poem the *Aeneid* refers to the Carthaginians as the
'double-tongued people of Tyre' (1.661). This was a nod not only to their
Tyrian origins but also to the multilingual traditions of the Carthaginians.
In Virgil's text, the underlying slur of bilingualism is employed to display the
duplicitous nature of the Carthaginians which was a common stereotype in
the Roman mind.

Carthage soon grew from being a small settlement on a hill facing the sea that we call the Byrsa to a grand and monumental city with a population that may have rivalled Alexandria and Antioch at its height in the third century BCE (although Strabo's claim (17.3.15) of seventy myriads of men – 700,000 – seems a mighty exaggeration). To what extent Carthage controlled an empire in this period (from the late ninth to the second centuries BCE) has been disputed over the centuries and the debate has received much attention in the last two decades. Research on the economics of Carthage has helped to determine not only what a Carthaginian 'empire' might have meant but also to shed light on the political and military structures that were part of the city's strategic preoccupation.[2] In origin, Carthage was one of many colonial foundations set up by city-states from the Levant that were linked by a common language, Phoenician. These Phoenician-speaking peoples came from a variety of places (for example, Sidon, Tyre and Byblos) that colonized the western Mediterranean in the ninth through seventh centuries BCE. They founded cities across the western Mediterranean: in Sicily, Sardinia, Corsica, the Balearic Islands, the Iberian coast of the Mediterranean and the Atlantic and all along the North African coast. At its height, from the fifth to the third centuries BCE, Carthage thus was at the centre of a broad network of city-states that were connected to each other through this shared language and culture.[3]

In this period, Carthage encompassed a large urban centre concentrated on the Byrsa hill, with attached agricultural land to the north and west (called the Megara) inside its strong defensive walls (see Map 1.2). It was, as far as we know, a city of temples and public areas, sophisticated urban planning, multi-storeyed buildings and industrial complexes.[4] The importance of the city as a cultural centre and maritime power grew over time and is best witnessed through the visible influence in material culture that extended to Sicily, Sardinia and Corsica, along the coast of North Africa and to the Balearic Islands and southern Iberian Peninsula. It was, in fact, on Ibiza that the Carthaginians may even have founded their first colony in the sixth century BCE. This early colonization is debated but comes from a statement in Diodorus Siculus (5.16), whose *Library of History* is one of our main sources for ancient Carthage. In the centuries after Carthage's ninth-century foundation, the western Mediterranean grew ever more crowded, with new urban foundations established by the Etruscans in Italy and other Phoenician-speaking peoples along with colonists from Greek-speaking city-states on both mainland Greece and in Asia Minor.

Carthage itself thrived due to its prime location, excellent agricultural land and prosperous maritime economy. The city grew to be the dominant urban force among many other cities with Phoenician origins, controlling the ports and trading routes through the central Mediterranean. In Sicily, where the many cultures of the island lived with and influenced each other, the Carthaginian cultural presence was centred on the west of the island,

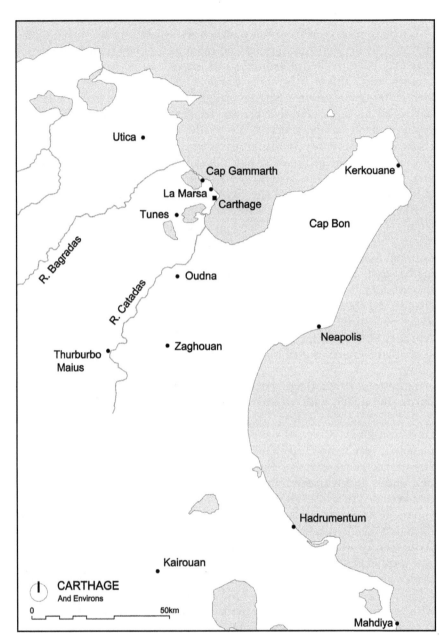

MAP 1.2 *Carthage and environs (drawn by Stephen Copp).*

with connected and allied ports at Panormus, Drepana, Mozia and then Lilybaeum (modern Palermo, Trapani, Mozia and Marsala). But the island also was an important point of contact, dialogue and conflict with the Greek-speaking population there and, for Carthage, would be crucial when it became the centre of the first of their epic wars with Rome (264–241 BCE).

As Carthage was growing and extending its influence from the sixth to the fourth centuries BCE, so too was the city of Rome. By the early third century BCE, the two most powerful city states in the western Mediterranean confronted each other across the narrow straits of Messina that separated Italy from Sicily. It would be the wars with Rome that came to define the history of Carthage in its first incarnation, in what is referred to as the Punic phase. The wars that we call the Punic Wars, after the Roman name for Carthaginian culture, were fought for dominance of the central and western areas of the Mediterranean, and this phase governs our understanding of the city in the Hellenistic world.[5]

It is only the Roman version of the wars with Carthage that has been preserved, with the Carthaginians' own stories long lost to legend and myth. Both Roman and Greek writers narrate the story and construct an epic environment where the two city-states fought total war for domination of the whole world. This, at least, is the tale told by the Greek historian Polybius (c. 200–118 BCE), who was a contemporary of the events and on whom later authors relied. The realities were, of course, slightly less global but it is important to understand that the Romans saw the war with Carthage as a fundamental part of their growth to empire. As a result, this has skewed the perspective, so that achieving a non-Roman view is virtually impossible.

For just over a century (from the middle of the third to the middle of the second centuries BCE), Rome and Carthage were engaged in warfare. Sicily was the flashpoint for the First Punic War (264–241 BCE), as each side vied for supremacy on the island. It was a close run and hard-fought war that involved epic naval battles around the island of Sicily and an invasion of Africa by the Romans. In the end, however, it would be manpower and financial difficulties that brought about a Carthaginian defeat. For Carthage, the First Punic War ended with the Treaty of Lutatius and the loss of their influence and allies on Sicily. These events were followed almost at once by a civil war back home (241–238 BCE). The financial crisis at the end of the war resulted in the inability of the Carthaginians to pay their mercenaries and allied soldiers who had fought for them against Rome. The Romans interfered in this conflict and, in particular, seized Sardinia from the Carthaginians, which would hasten the advent of what we call the Second Punic War (218–202 BCE).

The Second Punic War was a complex geopolitical struggle fought on many fronts and involving many of the powerful players in the wider Mediterranean, with key theatres in the Iberian Peninsula and across southern Italy. It would be a defining moment for both Carthage and its rival, Rome. The fighting took place mostly in the Carthaginian controlled Iberian Peninsula (modern Spain and Portugal) and in Italy. The war is often remembered for the famous crossing of the Alps by the general Hannibal with his elephants. Hannibal would go on to challenge the Roman state to its very core in the early years of the war (c. 218–212 BCE), most notably in the iconic battles at Lake Trasimene (217) and Cannae (216). By 206, the picture looked bleak for Rome, but the victory over Hannibal's brothers in the Iberian Peninsula and Hannibal's ever decreasing base of support in Italy meant that he was recalled to Africa in 202 BCE.

Carthage had been struggling to support its armies in both Spain and Italy and had faced raiding along its coastal regions. The Numidian neighbours of the Carthaginians, always important, soon became critical to their continued survival.[6] The final battle took place at Zama, now in central Tunisia, between Hannibal and the Roman general Scipio in 202 BCE. With Scipio's victory, the Carthaginians sued for peace. The conditions imposed by the Roman general were harsh. The city was to pay a fifty-year war indemnity to Rome and was forced to give up its military capacity almost in its entirety. The indigenous peoples of North Africa who had once allied and intermarried with the Carthaginians had switched sides to the Romans in the war. As a result, they gained the support of the Roman state and were rewarded with increased territorial autonomy at the expense of Carthage.[7]

The third and final conflict between Rome and Carthage (149–146 BCE) was an aggressive war on the part of the Romans. The period between the Second and Third Punic Wars had been one of surprising prosperity at Carthage. It was a time of urban growth and development, with many scholars proposing that the city thrived without the vast expense of having to support a military machine and with the increased connectivity across the Mediterranean in this period. Certainly, the development of the new ports that are still visible today was a symbol of this prosperity, as was the offer to pay off the entire indemnity just ten years after it was first imposed.[8]

This prosperity would end once the period of the war indemnity from the Second Punic War finished in 151 BCE. It did not take long for the Romans to goad their old enemy into taking the field and the century of conflict ended with the complete obliteration of the city of Carthage in 146 BCE after a three-year siege. Not all agreed with this policy at Rome. The Roman senator Cato the Elder is said to have repeated his mantra 'Carthage must be destroyed' (*delenda est Carthago*) at the end of every speech he gave in the senate, but his rival Scipio Nasica would retort 'Carthage must be spared' at the end of each of his own (Plut. *Cato the Elder*, 27). Although Cato died before the final end of Punic Carthage (after the Third Punic War), the result of the siege he so encouraged was that Carthage was burned to the ground and its population slaughtered or sold into slavery. The end of the first incarnation of Carthage was absolute and complete. These acts of destruction and the old Punic city of Carthage would occupy the minds of many Roman writers in the centuries that followed. Carthage became a moral lesson, a literary phenomenon, a canvas upon which the imperial Romans would cast their anxieties and aspirations.

One of the best descriptions of the topographical features of Carthage in this period comes from an eyewitness account of its final days. Passages from the second-century CE writer Appian are thought to preserve the original narrative of Polybius, who may have been present at the siege of the city. Appian's text (*Punica* 127–132) describes in gruesome detail how Roman troops had to fight their way, street by street, through Carthage while sweeping the dead and injured into mass graves, pushing on, day after day, to take and comprehensively destroy the city. The Romans moved from the grand ports northward to the public square of the agora and when reinforced by fresh troops they pushed on through the city (see Plan 1.1). In

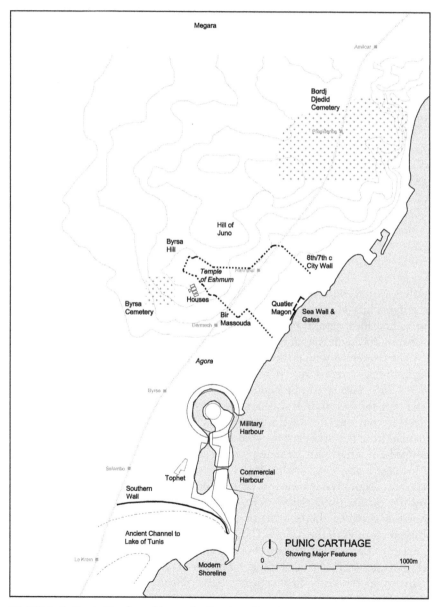

PLAN 1.1 *Punic Carthage (drawn by Stephen Copp).*

the agora the Roman soldiers entered the temple of Eshmun (called Apollo by Appian) and there found a statue of the god covered in gold and sitting in a shrine of beaten gold. Appian tells us they chopped it to pieces with their swords.

The Carthaginians fought bravely but were overcome. They took refuge on their citadel, the Byrsa hill. The Roman attack focused there and on the three streets that ascended from 'the agora to the citadel'. They 'captured the first few houses, and from them attacked the occupants of the next'. Timbers were lain across the narrow passageways and the soldiers crossed on these makeshift bridges. After the Roman soldiers had gained the top of the hill, we are told they set fire to the houses and the dense urban settlements leading up to the Byrsa hill. They must have watched from on high as the fire spread through the city. Appian records six days and nights of 'this kind of turmoil'.

Appian's graphic tale speaks of the death and destruction suffered by the Carthaginians and it also preserves some of the few bits of topographical detail of Punic Carthage that are nowhere else recorded. It is this description of the demise of Carthage that has helped to formulate an idea of the layout of the Punic city. These details would draw early archaeologists to the area in search of the urban landscape described in the text. The picture preserved is that of a metropolis on the Mediterranean with an elaborate sea wall and wide defensive land walls, a sophisticated dual port with military and commercial functions and ship sheds. There were multi-storeyed buildings lining the streets of a densely occupied core of the city, with monumental public spaces containing temples in the agora, right next to the ports, and on the Byrsa hill. The best-known and often employed image of Punic Carthage in its first incarnation – by the French/Tunisian artist Jean-Claude Golvin – is based on the description found in Appian (see Figure 1.1).

The degree to which the Punic city was destroyed is further brought to light by the late antique historian Orosius. Writing centuries later, in the early fifth century CE, he claims that Carthage burned for seventeen days and that the destruction was complete (*Hist.* 4.23). The Roman Senate had decreed that the site should be cursed and there was a prohibition against reinhabiting the area, but to what extent these orders were followed in the immediate aftermath remains a matter of speculation. The legend of Carthage being sown with salt has been proven to be of early modern, not ancient, origin. What is clear is that the burnt archaeological context created by the destruction, visible across excavations in the city, marks a clear horizon between the two major phases of occupation, the Punic and the Roman. Stories of the ruins at Carthage in the years following its destruction appear in the ancient sources. For example, Plutarch mentions the renegade Roman general Marius hiding from his rival Sulla's armies among the remains in the early first century BCE (*Marius*, 40.4) and the troops of Pompey the Great in 81 BCE searching for the buried treasure of the lost city (*Pompey*, 11).

FIGURE 1.1 *Punic city of Carthage (reconstruction by Jean-Claude Golvin).*

Once the original Carthage had been destroyed, a Roman resettlement was inevitable given the strategic location of the city in the Mediterranean and the fertility of the surrounding area. Rome's chaotic internal politics in the late second century and throughout the first century BCE only delayed the process. An attempt was made to found a colony named Junonia on the site of Carthage by the tribune Gaius Gracchus just twenty years after the city's destruction (Plut. *C. Gracchus*, 11). This was significant because, for the first time, the Romans had ventured to establish a colonial foundation beyond the borders of Italy, confirming the importance of the site. In 122 BCE, the sources claim that 6,000 settlers were sent to Carthage as part of Gracchus' plans for land redistribution. But the following year, when Gracchus was murdered in violent uprisings in Rome, the project faltered, though there is evidence that a land commissioner was still active there after Gracchus' death.[9]

Further attempts at colonization were made but the evidence is sketchy until the official refoundation of the city late in the first century BCE. This coincided with the rule of Octavian, Rome's victor in the civil wars of the late republic, who became the first emperor, Augustus. The impetus for establishing a settlement at the site had come from Julius Caesar, who had chosen Carthage as one of the places where the poor of Rome might be sent. Caesar's assassination put everything on hold again. Once in power, Octavian set out to fulfil his adoptive father's plans, with the intention of building a city at Carthage to rival that of its original counterpart. The official refoundation took place in 29 BCE. Named for the Julian family as *Colonia Concordia Iulia Karthago*, the new city would be known by its old name, Karthago (Plut. *Caesar* 57).[10]

Carthage was granted the status of a colony and, as such, Roman citizen settlers were sent to repopulate the city. Most of what we know of the urban landscape of Carthage comes from after this period, the era of the Roman Empire. This iteration of Carthage as a Roman Mediterranean city has left the biggest imprint in terms of material culture and architecture still visible at the site. As the so-called *Pax Romana* settled across the Mediterranean in the decades after Octavian won the civil war, the new city of Carthage thrived once more. It again became a major port and commercial centre in the middle of the Mediterranean, connecting to cities east and west. Carthage was eventually made the capital of the Roman province of Africa Proconsularis and the seat of the provincial governor. The new colony lay on top of the old, the city set out on an urban grid system with the axis, the meeting of the two main roads of the city (called by the Romans *decumanus maximus* and *cardo maximus*), lying at the very centre of the Byrsa hill (see Plan 1.2).[11]

We know from excavations at Carthage that re-establishing a city on the same site required some significant construction and alterations. The Romans completely reworked the topography of the Byrsa hill that had been the sacred and ceremonial centre of the Punic city. This massive Roman engineering project seems to have set out to erase any trace of the original buildings on the Byrsa that might have been left on the summit. The top of the hill was lopped off, and the summit flattened and widened. Tons of earth were moved to enlarge the space and brick-faced concrete supports were set deep into the slope of the hill. This newly constructed and enlarged area became the forum of the reborn city. Archaeologists working at Carthage over the last two centuries have uncovered both the Roman brick foundations for the central forum and the Punic houses with their built-in cisterns for water collection that lay beneath those foundations on the slopes of the Byrsa hill (see Figure 1.2). These remains are clearly visible in the brick pylons that lie around the foundation stones of the Punic houses when you visit today.

As the capital and seat of the governor, this new Carthage was fitted with all the trappings of a Roman imperial city. It took on these urban attributes over the course of the first two centuries CE, but there are indications that prosperity came very quickly. By the 40s CE, during the reign of the emperor Claudius, Carthage was described as having 'regained all its previous wealth' according to the ancient author Pomponius Mela (*Chor.* 1.34). It is from the second century that we can see impressive imperial monumentality being introduced to the city. A theatre and odeum were constructed as well as an amphitheatre of substantial size, seating approximately 30,000, and a circus with an estimated capacity of just under 70,000.[12] Large imperial baths were built in the middle of the second century CE under the patronage of the emperor Antoninus Pius, whose name they carry today. Modelled after imperial baths in Rome, they sat on a spectacular site on the coast and,

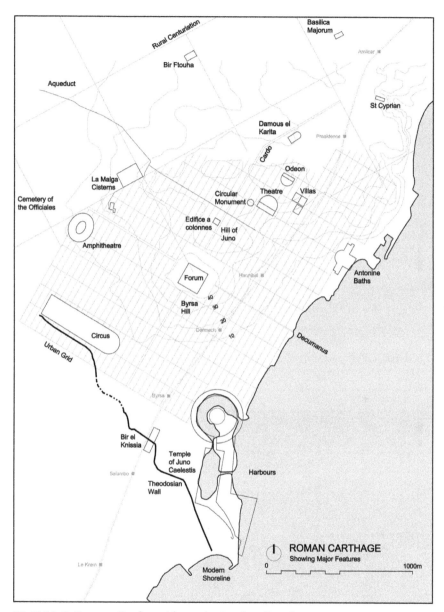

PLAN 1.2 *Roman Carthage (drawn by Stephen Copp).*

because of the location and their size, would have presented an impressive vista from the sea (see Figure 1.3). The Antonine baths are still the most impressive of the remains of Carthage visible to visitors today.

To accommodate the baths as well as the growing city, a major aqueduct running from a spring at Zaghoun, southeast of Carthage in the hills, was built in 120 CE (see Map 1.2). The estimated volume of water it carried, at

FIGURE 1.2 *Punic houses on the Byrsa hill (photo by Eve MacDonald).*

FIGURE 1.3 *The Antonine baths (photo by Eve MacDonald).*

32 million litres (roughly 7 million gallons) a day for a distance of some 90 kilometres, can give us some idea of the size and importance of the Roman incarnation of Carthage. The city also had one of only two units of urban cohorts found outside of Italy (the other was at Lugdunum, modern Lyon). The establishment of such a unit at Carthage is testament to the significance of the city in the eyes of the Romans. Its role was likely similar to those in other port towns (Puteoli, Ostia), namely to help maintain peace in the area and to ensure the safety of the grain supply.[13]

Though clearly appearing as a Roman city, Carthage in this period still retained a few traces of its earlier, Punic, existence. Most noticeable on the ground today are the ports (see Plan 1.2). The Romans reused the location, keeping the shape and the form of the late Punic ports, but constructing grand new buildings in the second century CE. As a monumental double-port system with an elaborately decorated commercial and military harbour, these structures were some of the most significant features of the city and any who approached Carthage from the sea must have been suitably impressed. By late in the second century CE, one source mentioned that a fleet had been set up at Carthage by the emperor Commodus in order to secure the important supply of food that came from the fertile agricultural lands around the city and in the hinterland of the province (HA, *Commodus* 17.7–8). From ceramic studies in Rome, we can surmise that much of the city's supply of olive oil by this time seems to have relied on African production. The new fleet was the first to be stationed at Carthage since the end of the Punic city almost 250 years earlier, although there is little evidence other than this comment in the *Historia Augusta*, which is notoriously unreliable.

The other notable imprint of the Punic city in Roman times was the Temple of Juno Caelestis. The Roman temple sat on the location of a Punic sanctuary and temple complex that is referred to as the Sanctuary or Precinct of Tanit, Sanctuary of Ba'al or the Tophet, as it is more commonly known. Located near the ports of the city, it occupied a central space in the urban landscape and had done so throughout all the various occupation phases. The Carthaginian name for this space used by the original inhabitants is nowhere recorded, but this had been the most sacred area of the Punic city and one of the very earliest public spaces. The Romans acknowledged its importance by building a temple that maintained continuity with the earlier use. The Tophet is the most famous and notorious of the archaeological sites at Carthage. Thousands of votive offerings have been excavated from this spot, dedicated by Carthaginian families in fulfilment of a vow (see Plan 1.1). The votive offerings held the cremated remains of infants and very young children as well as animals. These remains were deposited in urns and the offering was marked by a commemorative stone or stele, sometimes with an inscription (see Figure 7.2 in Chapter 7). The deposits date back to the foundation of the very first city of Carthage, and the Roman construction of the Temple of Juno Caelestis was perhaps a way of marking the importance of the site and its contribution to the prosperity of the city through the commemoration of a Romanized version of the goddess. In its Roman guise there were no more deposits of the cremated remains of infants, but the significance of the place, as a foundational feature of Punic Carthage, seems to have been retained. In Chapter 7 we consider the story of the discovery and significance of the finds at the Tophet.[14]

The economy of Carthage in the period of the Roman Empire was focused on agricultural wealth and the proximity of grain and other foodstuffs for the supply of Rome. As recent work has illustrated, the rich agricultural lands of Carthage's heartland had always been a key part of its prosperity, in both the Punic and Roman phases. Amphorae (containers for wine and oil) from Carthage can be tracked around the empire into the fourth and fifth centuries CE. This connectivity illustrates that the city retained its agricultural role and it would even go on to supply the new Rome – the eastern city of Constantinople – into the sixth and seventh centuries. Also important was the supply of wild animals for the hunting spectacles (*venationes*) held across the empire. There are a sizeable number of mosaics from North Africa, suggesting that the industrial capture of wild North African fauna was an important local industry, though more often this is believed to have been done by imperial soldiers.[15]

Although the third century CE was a time of political unrest and some chaos across the Roman Empire at large, life in Roman Carthage continued without too much disruption on a grand political scale. The city played a pivotal role in the rise of the Gordian emperors in 238 CE, though their power was short-lived. Otherwise, the area mostly escaped the turmoil that occurred elsewhere along the frontiers of the empire. Estimates based on public infrastructure and housing block numbers put the population of Carthage at perhaps as many as 300,000 people in this period. Such numbers are always difficult to estimate but if roughly accurate it would make Carthage easily the second largest city after Rome in the western empire. In addition, Carthage not only kept its importance but also emerged as the capital of the Diocese of Africa in the restructuring of the empire that occurred under the emperor Diocletian (285–305 CE).

In 1901, a publication by the historian Auguste Audollent, *Carthage Romaine*, provided an overview of the history, archaeology and context of the Roman city. In his introduction, Audollent noted that there were two distinct periods when the ancient literary sources focused on the city of Carthage: the Punic Wars with Rome in the third century BCE and the time when the Christian city was thriving, with Tertullian, St Cyprian and St Augustine all living there, from the second to fourth centuries CE. As a result, a broader picture of the people and stories of the city can be appreciated for those periods. Archaeologically, however, it is the imperial Roman city that has left the greatest impact at the site in terms of standing remains. The city's architectural monumentality can be envisaged by the grand theatre, amphitheatre, public spaces, circus, baths, luxurious hill-top villas and ports. But, as Audollent put it, historically Carthage rests 'in the shadows', the population largely anonymous during the period of the principate through to the high empire.[16] To a certain extent, we can visualize them through their spectacular mosaics, many of which were uncovered in the early years of archaeological excavation at Carthage. Occasionally, though, we also can hear their voices as celebrated in literature like that of Apuleius, who wrote in the early second century. In his *Florida* (20.10), he calls Carthage the celestial muse of Africa and waxes lyrically about Carthage as the instructress and inspiration for the Roman world.

Life in Roman Carthage is most often viewed, however, through the sources which describe the growing importance of the city as a centre for Christianity. There are rich details in the accounts of individuals living there. The Christian writer Tertullian lived in Carthage and wrote about the lives and troubles of its Christian community in the late second and early third centuries CE. The tradition of martyrdom, so important in the narrative of Christianity, is seen in the surviving accounts of the deaths of two young mothers from Carthage, Perpetua and Felicitas, in 203 CE.[17] This dramatic martyrdom is today commemorated with a pillar in the remains of the Roman amphitheatre where the deaths took place (see Figure 6.2 in Chapter 6). The fate of Carthage's controversial bishop Cyprian, who was martyred in the mid-third century CE, is chronicled in a biography as well as in extant letters. The traditions of Western Christianity were thus incubated at Carthage and culminated in the force that was St Augustine, who, as a young man, attended school and lived among the Carthaginians. His life spanned the late fourth and early fifth centuries CE and he wrote his *Confessions* at a time when the city was undergoing many political and physical changes.[18]

Christianity would have a significant impact on the topography and urban landscape of Carthage. The growth of the Christian community and development of the Church led to the construction of *basilicae* and *martyria*, first on the outskirts of the urban centre clustered around the ancient *necropoleis* (cemeteries) and then in the heart of the city (see Plan 1.2). Excavations have illustrated how public places were given over to spaces of Christian worship. The presence of Christian structures also shifted burial patterns. Many of the new structures were constructed by dismantling the traditional religious architecture and these stones then used to build the new. This process intensified over the fourth and fifth centuries as Christianity gained imperial power and authority. The Roman imperial city at Carthage was being recycled to create a new Christian urban space.[19]

In the fifth century CE, around 425, defensive walls once more appeared around Carthage. These were the first fortifications to be constructed since the Punic walls had been destroyed six centuries earlier. Excavations at Carthage in the twentieth century have provided some detail to allow the southern line of the wall to be mapped (see Plan 1.2). Called after the emperor who ruled in these years, the Theodosian Wall was built to guard against the increased threat of incursions from the Vandals, a Germanic people who had been on the move through mainland Europe and had crossed to Africa.[20] Despite these efforts to repel them, the Vandals took Carthage in 434 CE and dominated the city for the rest of the fifth century. The changes witnessed there in this period are emphasized in Roman literary sources, such as in the *Life of Augustine* by Possidius (chapter 28), which decry a social and cultural disaster arriving with the Vandals. In some ways, the Roman writers like to designate the Vandals as the 'heirs to perfidious Carthage', as Richard Miles has put it in a recent article.[21] What remains intriguing is how the Vandals also represented themselves as the heirs to Punic Carthage in a positive sense. This can be seen in the minting of coins with designs evocative of those of a much earlier period as well as the ways in which the Vandals made use of literature to promote *their* Carthage, most notably in the reign of Thrasamund (ruled 496–523 CE).[22]

The Vandal city was also embellished as befitted the capital of a kingdom rather than a province of empire, with a palace and other indicative changes to show its new status. In addition, a major change occurred in the sphere of religion. The new Vandal rulers, as Arian Christians, practised a different version of the Roman state Christianity and were considered heretical by many. Vandal churches were built or existing churches adapted to accommodate these differences in ritual and practice.[23] But, for the most part, the Vandals were content to make use of the monumental Roman buildings in Carthage, given that the grandeur only enhanced their capital city. In his description of the wars with the Vandals that occurred in the sixth century CE, the Byzantine writer Procopius likens the Vandals at Carthage to those who were softened by and succumbed to the luxuries of the place (Procop. *On the Wars* 4.9). A literary trope, this is a way of comparing the impact of the city and its very nature on the Vandals with the hardened indigenous peoples, the Moors. Nonetheless, the way Procopius portrays the Vandals as soft and indulgent, with tables filled with goods from the rich lands and sea of Africa, serves to emphasize the way that the richness of Carthage was a persistent characteristic of the city as described by others. New research on the diet of people buried in a Vandal period cemetery at Carthage may indicate some shifts in dietary practices in the sample population, including less consumption of seafood and fish than comparative populations, but any specific attributions to ethnicity remains difficult.[24]

Despite Procopius' accusations of excess and wealth, by the time the Byzantine general Belisarius conquered the region in the name of the emperor Justinian (536 CE), there had been a shift in the size and grandeur of the city. The economy had visibly shrunk. Grand public spaces were given over to small industries and agriculture. This was, it is worth emphasizing, a gradual process that had been taking place over the final centuries of the antique occupation of Carthage. It is mirrored in many other cities in the Mediterranean in the sixth and seventh centuries, as the ways of life were changing with less connectivity between regions. The concentration in the urban area of Carthage on small scale and local production of essential goods and services highlights these shifts.

Contemporary accounts of the sixth century CE describe a population in North Africa heavily exploited by Byzantine occupation and taxation so that by the time of the Arab Muslim conquests in the late seventh century CE, there was a much-diminished population at Carthage. The late Roman period population scattered, with some fleeing across the Mediterranean while others retreated to safer ground inland. Excavations at Carthage and other sites in North Africa tell us that much of the population had already shifted from urban to rural sites by this time. That anyone was at Carthage at all attests to its premium location. The maritime focus that had been the root of so much of Carthage's prosperity over the centuries would also turn out to be one of greatest vulnerabilities in terms of the preservation of the archaeological material at the site.[25]

2

From Carthage to Tunis

A New Focus

The creation of the archaeological site at Carthage is a result of the landscape, the geography and the post-antique history of North Africa. When ancient Carthage fell again in *c*. 696, 1,500 years after its original foundation and almost 850 years after its first fall, it had suffered from decades of Arab and Amazigh raids and attacks from the south. The Umayyad army under the command of their great general Hassan ibn al-Numan would eventually take the city, the Arabic historian Ibn Idhari al-Marrakushi claiming that the conqueror had the city destroyed and 'dismantled so that every trace was defaced'.[1] Scholars of the period question just how accurate this account is, as it seems to be influenced by the overriding narrative of earlier tales that told of the Roman destruction of Punic Carthage. As Walter Kaegi points out, this would put the Arab conquests of the famous city into the continuum of ancient epic histories. Carthage had indeed survived many incarnations extending back across the millennia but, by the time of the Arab conquest, it had already been much reduced in size and population, remaining an isolated outpost nominally ruled from an ever-distant and deeply unpopular eastern Roman capital, Constantinople.[2]

There was no longer a large urban population and many had abandoned the city, moved inland or fled across the sea to Sicily or to Spain. The victorious Umayyad army, based at their newly established capital of Kairouan (*c*. 670), had fought their way to the coast from the south to take Carthage. But the Umayyads never fully occupied Carthage, and other habitation there continued in one form or another. The battle for North Africa had been fierce and in no way an easy conquest for the Umayyads. Intense local resistance is exemplified by a woman known as Kahina, an indigenous leader and erstwhile 'prophetess', who led the fight in greater Numidia (a region here covering parts of both modern Algeria and Tunisia) against Hassan ibn al-Numan from 698 to 703. Like that of Dido in Tunisia, Kahina's legend lives on today among the modern inhabitants of Algeria and illustrates what a strong symbol of resistance and identity she provided (see Figure 2.1).[3]

FIGURE 2.1 *Statue of Kahina in Algeria (Wikipedia).*

Once the Arab Muslim conquest was complete, the new rulers chose to settle on the site of Tunes, an ancient city set a few kilometres to the south of Carthage. Tunis, as it became known, was better protected, set back from the coast and sheltered by a lake, while still with easy access to the sea (see Map 1.2 in Chapter 1). As the new foundation at Tunis flourished in the eighth century CE and grew to prominence in early Islamic North Africa, the remains of the ancient city of Carthage were further reduced to a suburban curiosity. From this moment onwards, the view of Carthage shifts and, in the early medieval period, it is through the optic of visitors to Tunis that the archaeological site at Carthage must be perceived.[4]

Today there is a growing body of archaeological evidence for early medieval North Africa from sites across the region that is changing our understanding of the period directly after the Arab conquests. The approach, in the nineteenth and into the twentieth century, was to disregard and even to destroy the early medieval (and sometime late antique) occupation layers at sites. Much of the material that might have been preserved at Carthage for this period was not of interest to archaeologists at the time and the early medieval residues at the site were cast aside in the quest for the even earlier cities, the Christian, Roman or Punic. The past thirty years has shifted this perspective and we have seen more and more scholarly publications in which previous archaeological excavations are re-evaluated to substantially broaden our understanding of this moment of transition. In 2002, volume ten of the journal *Antiquité Tardive* (Late Antiquity), focusing on Vandal and Byzantine North Africa, marked a turning point, with papers presenting evidence for a more substantial occupation at Carthage, immediately post-Arab conquest, than previously thought.[5] Although much of this evidence was destroyed, we now can say that elite Arabs settled in smaller locations across the remains of the city, occupying key strategic centres and prestigious buildings. Much of the monumental city of ancient Carthage that would have been visible at the time of the Umayyad conquests had been built in the second century CE when the Roman urban landscape had acquired its imperial baths, amphitheatre, theatre and circus. These impressive stone-built structures of the ancient city were then both occupied and also recycled over the subsequent centuries. In fact, the fortunes of ancient Carthage soon became closely linked with those of Arab Tunis, as the very stones of the old were built into the growing centre of the new city.

Complicating matters further in our understanding of this period is a scarcity of literary evidence. After 698 and throughout the early medieval period, little was recorded of Carthage. There are comments in a range of different sources, mostly Arab geographers who were curious and interested in the history of *Kartdjanna* (as it was called). The state of the visible remains in these fascinating early medieval accounts can help to piece together a few important details about the formation of Carthage as an archaeological site, although the views presented are often inconsistent. It was more than two centuries after Carthage fell that a scholar named Ahmed Ben Qali Mahalli records with some detail that there were 'beautiful constructions . . . splendid buildings in white marble topped with coloured statues representing men and all kinds of animals'. In the eleventh century, an Andalusian scholar, Abou Obeid el Bekri, provided a more detailed picture of Carthage in his work commonly known in English as the *Description of Africa Septentrionale* (published mid-eleventh century). Of the early medieval sources, his account is considered to be the most reliable, though it is thought that he never actually visited Carthage himself.[6]

What el Bekri wrote about the city was like a composite view of the standing ruins at Carthage that resulted from talking to contemporary visitors to Tunis. His eyewitnesses told him stories of what was left of this renowned location and he claimed that Tunis was 'the child of Carthage', declaring that the city had borrowed the marble of Carthage to adorn its buildings. That such an abundance of building material so readily at hand had been used in the construction of Tunis is not surprising. Yet despite all the recycling, el Bekri records that there were still standing ruins many storeys high in places. These included a site he describes as 'a palace, called *Moallaca*, distinguished by its high elevation and composed of vaulted galleries that form many levels and is set facing the sea'. El Bekri's description of this 'palace on the sea' may refer to the great imperial baths of Carthage built by the emperor Antoninus Pius in the second century CE and still some of the most impressive ruins of the city (see Figure 1.3 in Chapter 1). But it is perhaps more credible, given that the toponym *Moallaca* means 'suspended' or 'hanging', that el Bekri is referring to a building that once sat on the Byrsa hill, the highest elevation at Carthage and centre of the ancient cities. *Moallaca* may have been the remains of a substantial Roman basilica that once dominated the forum on the Byrsa. Other ruins described include a 'theatre' (more likely the amphitheatre), preserved to a number of levels with its entrances and windows decorated with sculpted animals. El Bekri also offers an insight into activity at the site when he tells us that 'the marble is so abundant at Carthage that even if all the inhabitants of *Ifrikiya* gathered there to carry off the stone elsewhere they could not accomplish their task'. The growing city of Tunis was being fed with material from Carthage but el Bekri also implies that those from much further afield used the site as a quarry for quality building materials as well.[7]

When the Norman king of Sicily, Roger II, commissioned the geographer and twelfth-century traveller Muhammed Ibn Muhammad el Idrisi to write a description of Africa and Spain, his evidence broadly confirmed what el Bekri had written. Carthage is described as a site of standing ruins where local chieftains occupy one part of the ancient city in an area surrounded by a wall of earth. In the mid-twelfth century, the dominant structure on the Byrsa hill, referred to as *Moallaca* by el Bekri and others, served as the base for an independent 'warlord' of the Banu Hilal people named Muhriz ibn Ziyad. His life has been the subject of a recent study by Matt King, who centres the activity and trade out of Carthage on this tribal chieftain, providing further insight into the way the ancient city was occupied – and dismantled – in the post-antique landscape.[8] El Idrisi's text also mentions enormous cisterns and more details are provided about the amphitheatre (although he too refers to it as a theatre). The building is a 'remarkable vestige of Roman construction . . . that does not have an equal in magnificence in the universe'. The size of the building and its circular form are noted, as is the composition 'of around fifty arches; each of these arcades is larger than thirty *empans* across . . .' (an *empan* measures slightly less than a foot). The additional decorative sculptures of men, animals and ships are enthused about as is the quality of the stone. El Idrisi's wondrous report claims he has never before seen marble of such diverse type and beauty, to the extent that he finds it beyond words. These marbles, he goes on to note, 'are transported to countries near and far and that no one leaves Carthage without loading considerable quantities of stone onto ships or other means. One can occasionally find marble columns of forty *empans* circumference.' El Idrisi's claim that the diameter of certain columns visible at Carthage was over 9 metres is certainly an exaggeration, but the work provides us with the sense of how Carthage and her buildings were perceived at the time and the wonder that the standing remains evoked.[9]

These accounts of Carthage in the early medieval period, while imprecise and prone to exaggeration, illustrate the way the site was being used and thought of. It was a place of curiosity for Arab-speaking scholars exploring their world and, in part, became a supply centre of materials for the wider Mediterranean. Building materials were not only used locally but were shipped to overseas markets as well. Tunis itself was a thriving commercial and mercantile centre of exchange in the early Middle Ages.[10] Connectivity flourished across the Mediterranean, east and west, between Tunis and the Islamic caliphates of Egypt and Spain. Even more substantial was trade north and south between Tunis and Sicily, Marseille and the Italian city-states of Venice, Genoa and Pisa, all of which would sign commercial treaties with Tunis over the following century. An early example, in 1157, is the Emir Abdallah b. Abd al-Aziz of Tunis, who wrote to the Archbishop of Pisa outlining articles of exchange between the two cities. These letters reveal that trade between the two centres was formalized and frequent.

Archaeologists working in Pisa have shown that the link between the two cities was firmly established by the twelfth century. The import and export of ceramics between Tunis and Pisa is well documented and it is likely that marble and other ancient building stones from Carthage were part of larger shipments of agricultural produce. This is the way that North African pottery had been transported in the Roman period, added as ballast to ships departing for ports all over the Mediterranean. So, in the early medieval period, Tunis was at the centre of a vibrant trading environment between European and Middle Eastern cities, and the recycled building stone from Carthage formed a part of that network of goods. On the other hand, the reuse of ancient materials was nothing if not opportunistic and went on throughout the whole of the Mediterranean and across Europe and the Middle East. An economic case for the exploitation of Carthage in this period reflects the reality of the connected Mediterranean in the early Middle Ages.[11]

Tunis started its post-ancient existence as the third city of the region, after Kairouan and Mahdiya, but by the thirteenth century it was established as the capital of a new kingdom (see Map 1.2 in Chapter 1). Mahdiya had suffered a decline after being sacked during the turmoil that preceded the Almohad conquest of North Africa in the twelfth century. The Almohad caliphate had originated in the Atlas Mountains and ruled the region of al-Andalus and the Mahgreb (southern Spain and western North Africa from Tunisia to Morocco). At Tunis, a new dynasty known as the Hafsids had first been installed by the Almohads as governors in 1207. They then built their own state from that base and ruled independently from 1229 to 1574. The founder of the dynasty, Abu Zakariya, declared independence from the Almohads in 1229. By 1249, Muhammad al-Mustansir had adopted the title of caliph and ruled his own kingdom, with Tunis as its capital. The Hafsids were ethnically Amazigh and came to power at a crucial time for Tunis and the region. The city became the centrepiece of their prosperous and strategic kingdom which linked the Middle East and the western Mediterranean, southern Africa and Europe.[12]

A contemporary writer, al Abdari, enthusiastically expressed this view, calling Tunis 'a point of convergence for the sight of all, a rendezvous for voyagers from the east and the west'.[13] Five hundred years after the fall of Carthage, Tunis was connecting the medieval Mediterranean in a similar way to its ancient predecessor. The change in status at Tunis and the growth that accompanied this shift and expanding connectivity must have hastened the demolition of the ancient buildings at Carthage. There was a marked population growth in the thirteenth century and an ever-expanding need for even more building materials. This again emphasizes Carthage's seaside location and the ease with which the ruins could be quarried. The claim by a contemporary geographer, Ibn Said Gharnati, that Carthage was deserted by his day only proves that all these observations are a matter of perspective. What we can say is that the visible ruins at Carthage in the early medieval period were part of a multi-use site. Arabic and Mahgrebi scholars and travellers curious about the famed location of the ancient city visited, while both agricultural production and industrial activity occurred in places around the site.

In the summer of 1270, early in the era of the Hafsids, King Louis IX (later known as Saint Louis) of France attacked Tunis in a desultory and wayward military expedition that is known as the Seventh Crusade. The focus on Tunis as a target for crusading Europeans only emphasizes how prosperous the city must have been at the time. Reports tell us of the king and his Christian army watering their horses at the cisterns of Carthage and taking refuge behind the still-standing city walls that had been constructed by another Christian leader, the Roman emperor Theodosius II. These fifth-century CE fortification walls must have been solid enough to be useful – and clearly were too well constructed to have yet been mined for building materials. The French soldiers blocked up gaps and dug a deep ditch to increase the defensive capabilities of the ancient walls. Louis died suddenly in August 1270 at Carthage and his body was buried on the Byrsa hill at the very centre of the site of the ancient city (see Figure 2.2). Although his heart was taken away and buried in the Cathedral at Monreale on Sicily, the presence of the bones of the sainted king would have profound implications for the archaeological site of Carthage centuries later. These saintly remains would become of deep interest to the early French colonial archaeologists who came to Carthage and merged with the interests of missionary Christians.[14]

With Louis dead, his army abandoned their siege and returned across the Mediterranean. The caliph of Tunis, the famed al Mustansir, decided that any future invading force should be dissuaded from relying on the defences of ancient Carthage and he ordered the walls to be destroyed to their very foundations. This demolition, which coincided with another growth spurt of the new capital of the nascent kingdom, saw the wall broken down and usefully employed in the many other buildings being constructed in Tunis at the time. The story of the failed siege and the details of its aftermath were written about by Tunis' most famous son, Ibn Khaldun (see Figure 2.3). Born in Tunis in 1332 and a prolific thinker, Ibn Khaldun wrote history and philosophy while acting as a diplomat. He was also an intrepid traveller. As

FIGURE 2.2 *Statue and grave of St Louis on the Byrsa hill (photos by Sandra Bingham).*

an author and scholar, Ibn Khaldun's writings are still essential for contemporizing the Islamic societies of the time and the worlds they grew out of. He was also key in articulating a broader Islamicate view that the ancient cities of the pre-Islamic worlds were there to be contemplated and learned from. Martin Devecka's book, *Broken Cities*, points out that Ibn Khaldun saw the remnants of the ancient societies of the Mediterranean as a means to frame the past and the present. This framing of the ancient world provided a context that allowed Ibn Khaldun's contemporary readers to view and understand the ancient ruins.[15]

Part of the story Ibn Khaldun tells in his *Universal History* is of growing up in Tunis and bearing witness to its relationship with ruined Carthage. It is he who implies that the ancient walls at Carthage were substantial enough to still be useful in the thirteenth century and he describes family trips to the nearby site when he was a child. He tells us that in his day at Carthage there were 'the arcades of a building called Moallakah'. That same building,

FIGURE 2.3 *Ibn Khaldoun on the Tunisian 10-dinar note (Alamy).*

already mentioned by el Bekri in the eleventh century, is still dominant in the landscape in the fourteenth. Ibn Khaldun also notes that when the

> . . . [when] inhabitants of Tunis need stones the masons appreciate those from al Moallakah. They have for a long time tried to take it apart but an enormous effort is needed to detach even a small fragment of stone. People gather there for this work and I often witnessed it in my youth.

This story of youthful trips to Carthage is fascinating for the engagement it reveals with the site by the population of Tunis and also gives the impression that piece-by-piece and stone-by-stone, in wagons, carts and by ship, the visible ruins at the city of Carthage were being taken apart and taken away.[16]

In the sixteenth century, Tunis once again became the focus of a broader geopolitical narrative that would feature the site of ancient Carthage as a location. Tunis was still a thriving and multicultural place with a busy commercial port and central location in the Mediterranean at the time. For exactly this reason, it was caught up in the geopolitical battle for Mediterranean dominance between larger powers of the day. Throughout much of the century, rival fleets of the Holy Roman Emperor Charles V and the Ottoman Sultan, Suleiman the Magnificent, vied for control of the Mediterranean seaways and commerce. Although contemporary references to Carthage during this period are rare, they usually turn up in the context of war over the city of Tunis. Spanish troops held Tunis only for a short time, but even so, they took every opportunity to symbolically connect their conquest of Tunis to that of the Roman conquest of Carthage. We can see this in the tapestries commissioned by Charles V that celebrate his brief conquest of the region. The woven narrative creates a scene that depicts the Holy Roman Emperor of the sixteenth century as the legendary Roman Republican general Scipio Africanus. This would become a consistent idea in the European engagement with North Africa from the early modern period onwards, a concept modelled on ancient paradigms of wars between Carthage and Rome that would hold firm across the coming centuries.[17]

In reality, we know little about what was happening at the site of Carthage as control of Tunis – and especially its strategic port of La Goulette – shifted back and forth between the great powers. Tunis fell in 1534 to the Ottoman admiral Khayr-ad-din Barbarossa and then again in 1535 to Andrea Doria, the Genovese admiral and commander of Charles V's fleet. The armies of Charles V are reported to have laid waste to the villages that existed on the site of Carthage, which confirms that people were still living there at this date. Ottoman forces regained Tunis in 1569 but lost it again after the Battle of Lepanto in 1571. After taking Tunis again, Don Juan, the son of Charles V, also evoked the rivalry between Rome and Carthage by immediately riding out to Carthage. Ultimately, the Ottoman forces regained control, this time more permanently, in 1574 when a force led by the famed Sinan Pacha captured the city.[18]

Over this century of conflict, our main witness to the site of Carthage is a man known as Leo the African. Born Wasan ibn Muhammad al-Wazzan, his family was originally from Granada and when it fell in 1492, they fled across the Mediterranean to Fez. Leo grew up in Fez and was in the employ of the Wattasid Sultanate (1472–1554), travelling across North Africa, Asia and the Near East as their envoy. The author was captured by pirates in 1518, possibly off the coast of the island of Djerba, and sold into slavery in Italy. He was presented to Pope Leo X in Rome and spent time in the Castel Sant Angelo. Once he had converted to Christianity, Leo's release from captivity was secured and he took the Christian name John Leo (Giovanni Leone) in honour of the Pope. Leo the African's most famous book, *Descrittione del'Africa* (Description of Africa), was completed by 1526, which is the date of the only surviving manuscript. It was read widely by a contemporary audience: by 1556, there was a Latin, French and two Dutch versions of the text and by 1600 an English translation. The translation into European vernacular languages illustrates a fascination with the non-European world of North Africa and the Near East among an educated European population already by that stage engaged in laying in colonial foundations in North and South America.

Leo's work would continue to be deeply influential among European scholars as well, with key figures such as Edward Gibbon citing him as one of the sources for Carthage in his *Decline and Fall of the Roman Empire*, published in 1776. In his book, Leo describes Carthage as 'the famous and ancient city' and mentions an aqueduct and ruined walls, but he does not describe any other architectural features and includes few details of other ruins. The city of Carthage, from Leo's viewpoint, was still inhabited although it had sunk 'mighty low, containing about 500 sorry houses and not above 25 shops'. Its agriculturally rich location is confirmed again by the description of 'gardens covering the west and south parts of the city' that provided fruit sold at Tunis. That the aqueduct was still standing is made clear from its frequent appearance on contemporary maps and other media that depict the Ottoman and Spanish sieges of Tunis in the sixteenth century (see Figure 2.4).[19]

From this scattering of eyewitness accounts, we can see a dialogue among contemporaries that illustrates a fascination with the ruins of the ancient city. It also seems probable that most of the standing ruins described by el Bekri in the eleventh century had been cleared from the surface by the mid-sixteenth century. Political and social developments at Tunis during the medieval and early modern era had brought massive disturbance and

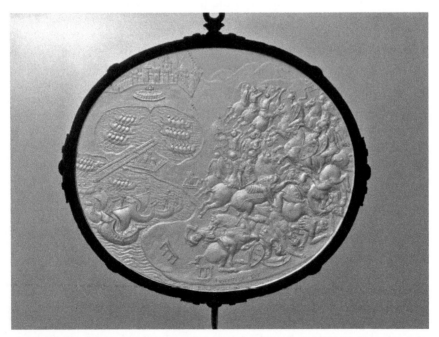

FIGURE 2.4 *Rock crystal image of the Battle of Tunis, c. 1544 by Giovanni Bernardi da Castel Bolognese, showing the ancient aqueduct at the bottom (Metropolitan Museum of New York).*

upheaval, as the ancient ruins were reused both near and far as building materials. But it must be acknowledged that the differences between the accounts of the ruins at Carthage by el Bekri and later by Leo are also a matter of perspective and expectation. In the Rome of Leo's time, much of the ancient imperial city was still partially visible and buildings like the Colosseum were still standing. By comparison, there was very little to see at Carthage. This also reflects a universal truth about visitors and witnesses to Carthage across the millennia: that what they thought of the site depended on what they wanted to find there. Many went away disappointed.

With the rise of a specific European fascination with the ancient world and the development of antiquarianism in the seventeenth century, the ruins of Carthage, or perhaps more specifically the *idea* of Carthage, was increasingly an object of interest. Carthage was well enough known that Shakespeare could use it as a reference in *The Tempest*. In Act 1, Scene 2, the stranded shipmates in a magical land exclaimed that 'this Tunis, sir, was Carthage'.[20] The tragedy of Dido and Aeneas also proved popular. It was turned into a play by Christopher Marlowe, *Dido: Queen of Carthage* (1593), and an opera by Henry Purcell, *Dido and Aeneas*, composed sometime in the 1680s, itself perhaps influenced by an earlier opera by Cavalli (*Didone* (Dido), 1640). The stories of the ancient city became even more entrenched in the popular imagination when the ancient Roman authors Livy and Virgil became widely available through translations into the vernacular languages of Europe. Virgil's *Aeneid* had been translated into French and Italian in the early seventeenth century and then into English by John Dryden in 1698. Livy was translated into English in the early seventeenth century. Both brought the stories of Carthage to a wider audience. During the sixteenth and seventeenth centuries, then, European popular culture increasingly embraced the stories and legends of Carthage and Rome.

By the seventeenth century, a European awareness of Carthage became fashionable as the political situation in the Mediterranean shifted and people became even more connected between the northern and southern shores of the sea. There was wider knowledge, more travel and also more turmoil as the Mediterranean became the focus of further geopolitical struggles and of the expansionist ambitions of rising nations such as England and France. Many of the European visitors to Carthage in the seventeenth century were not there by choice and had first come to the region as prisoners of the so-called Barbary pirates. Barbary is the name given to the kingdoms of North Africa – that is, Tripoli, Tunis and Algiers – that had been loosely under the rule of the Ottoman sultan since the late sixteenth century. While Morocco maintained its independence, it is also labelled with this epithet. Some of the individuals captured by the pirates and sold into slavery, on being freed, decided to stay in North Africa and converted to Islam. Among these were nascent antiquarians whose interests led them to explore Carthage. Others, who had arrived to negotiate the release of prisoners and visited Tunis under the protection of a Crown or the Church, would also contribute to the knowledge of the site. One early example of an eyewitness description of Carthage in this period is that of Father Pierre Dan, the head of the Mathurin (Trinitarian) brotherhood at Fontainebleau. He departed on a mission to ransom captives in the 'Barbary' kingdoms in 1634 and, upon his return in 1637, published his history of the region. Entitled *History of Barbary*, it proved popular enough to be reprinted in 1649. Father Dan's remarks – that there was nothing left at Carthage except a few bits of old masonry and that the site was now covered with orchards that bore lovely fruit – reinforces the idea that the monumental ancient buildings had all but disappeared.[21]

A more concerted interest in the site and ruins of Carthage in modern European accounts is exemplified by the correspondence of a French man who spent several years at Tunis in the early seventeenth century, first as a captive and then by choice. Born in 1568 in Rouen, Thomas d'Arcos was captured by pirates when he was in his early fifties and taken to Tunis. His intriguing career is a snapshot of the world of seventeenth-century travel and connectivity. It is rumoured that d'Arcos had spent time as a spy for the English at the end of the sixteenth century and had also been imprisoned in Rome in 1601. As a kind of seventeenth-century double agent, d'Arcos frequently travelled around the Mediterranean and it appears that he was captured early in 1625 on one of his many trips. A ransom was paid in April of that year by a friendly merchant, but despite being freed, d'Arcos did not leave Tunis after his release and instead became acquainted with the bey (the ruling Ottoman representative), taking on the role of advisor.[22]

While in Tunis, d'Arcos continued his correspondence with friends back in France and, in a letter of 1630 to Honoré Aycard, he described seeing 'bones thought to be those of a giant'. The letter was shown to one of Aycard's acquaintances, Nicolas-Claude Fabri de Peiresc, a magistrate and cleric, who had an interest in antiquarian matters. A decade earlier, Peiresc had heard about ancient inscriptions found near Tunis, which had piqued his curiosity about the area. Peiresc viewed d'Arcos as a useful contact, who could relay information about the area and report on any remarkable discoveries. The magistrate's interests in the ancient Mediterranean were wide-ranging, with a particular objective of creating a map of the region. With this in mind, Peiresc reached out to contacts in various locations throughout the Mediterranean to be his sources for the mapping project. With Carthage, he thought that the site ought to be considered as an equal to Rome, given its antiquity and history. Yet, with still so little known about the city other than the information from the ancient literary sources, Peiresc, in his empirical thinking, wanted to match what the sources said with what was on the ground. In d'Arcos, he had found the contact he needed. The correspondence between Peiresc and d'Arcos, conducted mainly through their mutual friend Aycard, reveals a fascinating relationship and gives an insight into many of the cultural issues of the day. The Christian Peiresc was troubled by d'Arcos' conversion to Islam in 1632 even though it was common for European captives in the Barbary kingdoms to convert (as it was for Muslim captives in Christian Europe, as noted with Leo the African above). This was especially true if they wanted to live in the area after gaining their freedom. D'Arcos' conversion would have offered him greater independence to operate across the region and around Tunis. In their correspondence, d'Arcos seems to have reassured Peiresc that he had not turned his back on all his Christian traditions. We get a glimpse here of how adept d'Arcos was at playing all sides, an essential skill for a European convert living and working at the court of the bey of Tunis.[23]

The published letters between the two correspondents, dating between 1630 and 1637, reflects the growing fascination of seventeenth-century Europeans with the material culture of antiquity in general. Scholars and amateurs were keen to collect antiquities and also curious about the city and culture of ancient Carthage. As noted above, Peiresc was interested in the topography of the site, especially in conjunction with the descriptions in the ancient sources. D'Arcos sent sketches and detailed drawings of Carthage, which Peiresc then annotated and correlated with the descriptions from those ancient sources. This is perhaps the very first attempt at providing an idea of what was on the ground, a topography of the ancient city. What is even more remarkable is how advanced the ideas of Peiresc were in respect of his view of the artefacts themselves. In the letters, he encouraged d'Arcos to apply scientific rigour to his approach. For example, Peiresc did not seek the actual stones that were inscribed, but he instructed d'Arcos on how to make squeezes so that there could be no mistaking what was on the stones. Other advice included studying everything in situ, to make copies, to be precise and to write field reports. All sound advice, even today.

On the other hand, d'Arcos for his part seemed more interested in the extraordinary and wonderful, such as the 'bones of the giant', much to the frustration of Peiresc (who had recognized the bones to be those of an elephant). D'Arcos often sent Peiresc curiosities, such as chameleons, instead of what had been asked of him (the chameleons did not survive the French winter). Peiresc's irritation with d'Arcos is clear in some of the letters, when his man on the ground appeared to be dragging his feet in getting the information that Peiresc wanted or was sending him information that was unhelpful. In fact, it may well be that d'Arcos himself grew tired of the persistent demands made by Peiresc, especially when it was difficult to provide what was being asked for given what little was visible at the site. D'Arcos was still in Tunis when Peiresc died in 1637. What emerges most clearly from the correspondence between these two men is how little available knowledge there was of Carthage in Europe beyond the ancient literary sources. Also clear is how discoveries on the ground could invoke an insatiable curiosity about the ancient city.[24]

The seventeenth century at Carthage was a time when stories and legends of the ancient city continued to fascinate European antiquarians and politicians – often one and the same. The visit of an Italian doctor named

Giovanni Pagni to the ruling bey of Tunis, Mourad II, in 1677 provides a final example. Pagni had been sent by the Grand Duke of Tuscany after the bey had requested medical help with an illness that his own doctors could not explain. Pagni was a multi-talented professor of medicine at the University of Pisa with a keen interest in antiquities and Latin epigraphy. During the year he spent in Tunis, he received more than twenty inscriptions from the Punic and Roman periods that mostly came from the area around Carthage. These were gifts from a grateful, and cured, bey and would form the basis of a collection in Florence that became available for scholars to study. The gifts reveal the steps being taken that furthered the dissemination of artefacts from, and interest in, ancient Carthage and North Africa. From this time forward, curiosity about Carthage and its antiquities would grow steadily in conjunction with European political interference in the region.[25]

3

The Europeans

By the time the urbane nineteenth-century writer, academic and orientalist François René de Chateaubriand was delayed at the port of La Goulette near the site of ancient Carthage in 1806 and 1807, he could write about a place 'crowded with the greatest memories of history'. These sentiments illustrate just how high expectations ran in the eighteenth and nineteenth centuries when Europeans first began to search in earnest for ancient Carthage. Much to the chagrin of these intrepid Englightenment minds, however, there was almost universal disappointment when the early visitors realized that the visible remains of Carthage did not live up to their expectations. In the late eighteenth century, the French botanist and naturalist René Louiche Desfontaines visited Carthage on a voyage to Tunis and Algers. Desfontaines categorically dismissed the site: 'The ruins at Carthage do not offer anything of interest: three big cisterns, the debris of an aqueduct, a few old walls, and stones piled up here and there in the countryside is all that remains of this famous rival of Rome.' So comprehensive was the destruction, that Edward Gibbon would claim, in the late 1780s, that 'the ruins of Carthage have perished; and the place might be unknown if some broken arches of an aqueduct did not guide the footsteps of the inquisitive traveller'.[1]

As the study of antiquity and antiquities developed in Europe, interest in North Africa encouraged a succession of Europeans to make the journey and explore Carthage. In the eyes of European travellers, this once great ancient city had been laid low and the events between the end of the seventh century CE – the last incarnation of ancient Carthage – and the eighteenth century had been so destructive to the physical site that there was little left to see. The narrative of ruin was not helped by the fact that cities of comparative size and legend, Athens and Rome, still had sufficient remains to feed the imagination of the early modern Europeans. Carthage, in contrast, had all but disappeared above ground.

Across all accounts of this period we see the same sense of disappointment at the state of the ruins at Carthage.[2] Much to the dismay of those who sought a comparison with Athens or Rome, at Carthage there was no Colosseum, no Parthenon – her secrets were going to be much more difficult to extract. At a practical level we have seen that the once 'perfect' port location of the original Phoenician city left it exposed and vulnerable in a post-ancient Mediterranean. The early travellers who record their disenchantment in letters and publications from the period were lamenting the lack of any standing ruins to inspire the imagination. They sighed over a barren landscape that once housed a city that ruled its own empire and had been the third largest city in the Roman Empire.

Key to this narrative is also a deeply rooted European prejudice against the contemporary inhabitants of North Africa. Whether as Muslims or as ethnically Arab/Ottoman/African or Amazigh peoples, they were held accountable for the state of the site, if not explicitly then implicitly. There was little European regard at the time for the vibrant metropolis of Tunis while these vivid descriptions of decay at Carthage are repeated across many examples. These portrayals are literary tropes employed frequently by those trying to assert a European cultural dominance in the region. Such a lament would become a fundamental part of the European colonial narrative that would serve to disassociate the inhabitants of the region from the ancient past across North Africa.[3] This is especially true once colonial and protectorate status was imposed in the nineteenth century. Then it would be European powers seeking to establish a link between their policies and a perceived ancient Roman and Christian glory. This view would deeply influence the understanding of and development at the archaeological site of Carthage for more than two centuries.

European powers and their engagement with the Ottoman Empire dominate the overarching geopolitical narrative in North Africa in these years. Ottoman rule in North Africa, and at Tunis specifically, lasted from the final conquest by Sinan Pacha in 1574 through to the establishment of French rule in 1883. Tunis became an *eyālet* to the Ottoman state; that is, a province that was ruled by semi-autonomous dynasties, the leaders of which were known by the title of bey.[4] The early years of European research and archaeological observations at Carthage took place over the period of the beylical dynasty of the Husaynids, who ruled from 1705 through to 1881. As noted in the previous chapter, Ottoman North Africa was referred to in the contemporary European and American parlance as the region of Barbary. The so-called Barbary pirates, or perhaps 'privateers' is a better description, sailed privately-run ships across the Mediterranean under the loose protection of one or another of the North African kingdoms. By the late eighteenth and nineteenth centuries, privateering was common across all nations and states in the Mediterranean and Atlantic as part of the larger struggle for colonial conquest and regional competition. The political and diplomatic engagement between the European powers and Tunis in these years often took place in the context of dealing with this 'issue', alongside the fall out around privateers and the resulting capture of individuals who might be ransomed.

Most of the voluntary travellers who came to Carthage did so with some kind of official position, either as representatives of the rulers of France or

England or of the Church. Edward Stanley's eighteenth-century publication certainly focused on the perceived perils of travelling in the region for a European gentleman: 'the want of places of refreshment on the roads, and the danger of venturing far inland among a set of barbarians ever intent on murder and rapine, are great discouragements to the inquisitive'.[5] Despite the perceived hardships faced by these gentlemen, a residual effect of the travelling and contact was that useful information about the state of the ruins at Carthage and an accurate guide to the region slowly began to form over the course of the eighteenth century. The beginnings of a modern conception of the urban landscape of ancient Carthage dates to this period.

One of the first to visit the area in the early eighteenth century was Thomas Shaw, the Anglican chaplain at Algiers, who made a short visit to Tunis in 1727. His *Travels or Observations*, published in 1738, holds a unique place in the study of Carthage. Shaw's is the earliest publication to make specific claims about the topography of the ancient site and is the first early-modern step towards a tangible mapping of the city (apart from the attempts made by Thomas d'Arcos on behalf of Peiresc, discussed in Chapter 2). Shaw offered views on two issues that would form the great debates in Carthaginian archaeology in the nineteenth century, namely the location of the most famous landmarks of the ancient city as described in the ancient sources: the ports and the Byrsa hill. In doing so, he provided a baseline from which others could work. Shaw turned out to be correct in his conjecture as to which of Carthage's hills was the Byrsa, but he erroneously placed the Punic ports at the basin of the Bagradas river, north of the site of Carthage and up the coast at Cap Gammarth (see Map 1.2 in Chapter 1).[6] That the location of these sites was in dispute is testimony to how little of ancient Carthage had survived above ground. In fact, through to the early twentieth century, the location of the Byrsa hill, the centre of the ancient city, would still being contested by various scholars. One wonders whether the medieval French soldiers who had buried their sainted king Louis IX on that hill recognized it was the Byrsa, or had just chosen the highest point in the vicinity?

Revolution in the Americas and France and a broader political and social upheaval across the Mediterranean took place at the end of the eighteenth and in the early nineteenth century. These events coincided with an increasing interest in archaeology and heritage across the Mediterranean and brought ancient Carthage into focus. This was especially true as the most renowned of ancient Carthaginians came to the fore of popular imagination. In 1801, the French painter David created his equestrian portrait of *Napoleon Crossing the Alps* on his way to the Battle of Marengo. David consciously evoked the memory of the Carthaginian general Hannibal whose name, along with that of Charlemagne, is engraved on the rocks at the foot of Napoleon's horse. In addition, images used in Joseph Turner's *Hannibal Crossing the Alps*, painted in 1812, were inspired by the Napoleonic wars but based on Carthaginian history. As France and England became rival nations whose conflict spread across the Mediterranean and the Near East

and into Asia and North America, both sides evoked the epic battles of
Roman and Carthaginian history in telling their stories. Turner would return
to Carthaginian history in his famous work, *Dido building Carthage* (1815),
in which he depicts a fantasy construction of the Punic city by the Phoenician
queen, Dido (see Figure 3.1).[7]

Carthage became a theme by which to contemporize geopolitical
struggles, as these few examples help to illustrate. The result was to bring an
increased awareness of the city into the minds of Europeans at a time when
archaeological investigation at the site was beginning in a real sense. The
objective of visitors to Carthage began to shift in these years from those who
travelled and visited sites out of curiosity to those who approached the
ancient world to conduct more scientific observations in the late eighteenth
and early nineteenth centuries. It was in search of the city of Hannibal and
Dido that the early nineteenth-century archaeological enthusiasts were
drawn to the site of Carthage. And it would again be events at Tunis that
would become the catalyst for archaeological activity at Carthage. What
might be called the inauguration of scientific research and the first steps
towards archaeology at the site was due to a multicultural group who
worked there in the early years of the nineteenth century. Each character
came to Tunis for very different reasons and all added to the knowledge and
development of research at Carthage and to the dissemination of
understanding of the material culture and history there. This eclectic group

FIGURE 3.1 Dido building Carthage *by J. M. W. Turner (© The National Gallery London).*

included a Dutch officer, an Italian priest, the Danish consul to Tunis, a noble Italian Napoleonic soldier and a French academic.

In 1786 the bey of Tunis was Ali Ben Hussein Ben Ali (ruled 1782–1814), who is known as Hammouda Bey. In the spirit of revolution and 'freedom' that filled the late eighteenth century world, he had broken away from his Ottoman overlords in a bid for independence. The Ottoman sultan, Abdulhamid I, sent a fleet to punish his rebellious bey, and the port fortress of La Goulette was bombarded and destroyed (see Map 1.2 in Chapter 1). La Goulette was key to guarding the port and inner harbour that fed the busy city of Tunis and features prominently in illustrations going back as far as the sixteenth century. In the years that followed the bombardment, Hammouda Bey reached out to various European nations for help in establishing an independent state. Following the upheaval brought about by the American and French revolutions, Tunisia developed commercial treaties with (among others) Napoleonic France, Spain and the newly formed United States. A request for aid in reconstructing the port at La Goulette was also made by the government at Tunis to the newly formed Batavian Republic (as the Netherlands was then known).[8]

In March of 1796, a Dutch officer named Jean Emile Humbert, an engineer in the army engineering corps, boarded a ship bound for Tunis accompanied by his regimental colonel, August Frank, and the colonel's son. Their project was to repair the port and fortress at La Goulette. The work on the port would continue for a decade while it was modernized and rebuilt. In 1806, Colonel Frank and his son returned to the Netherlands but Humbert remained behind, having accepted the post of Chief Engineer to the bey, which he occupied until 1819. Humbert's day job was to modernize the infrastructure of the city of Tunis and to increase the effectiveness of its fortifications. His favourite hobby, however, was archaeological research and antiquities. This meant that for almost twenty-five years, Humbert was able to turn his energies towards this passion and to methodically begin to map out and assess the standing ruins at ancient Carthage. For the Dutch, Humbert remains a hero of archaeology, so much so that in 2016, the then Prime Minister of the Netherlands, Mark Rutte, was able to claim, 'like some early-nineteenth-century Indiana Jones, Jean Emile Humbert put ancient Carthage on the map, both literally and metaphorically'.[9]

There is no doubt that Humbert's work at Carthage would have a profound influence on the development of research at the site. Contemporary accounts of all those who visited and wrote about the ruins at Carthage in this period mention 'the Dutch engineer'. His role was as a guide, local expert and technical assistant. Humbert often escorted visitors around Carthage, and his tours, as recorded by an English visitor to the site, included subterranean picnics in the Roman cisterns and songs about Queen Dido as part of the package. Humbert's work and research is one of the cornerstones for our current knowledge of the archaeological site. He engaged in excavations, mapped the area and measured locations for topographical research. All these together changed our understanding of Carthage. He was also a key influence on other researchers and investigators at Carthage at that time. This means that his views and ideas on Carthage were taken up in a number of publications from the first two decades of the nineteenth century and these further confirm his influence.[10]

A contemporary picture of what was happening on the ground at Carthage can be found in the writing of a man named Felice Caronni. He was a Barnabite priest from Milan who was captured by pirates while travelling on a ship out of Palermo on 9 June 1804. The story of Father Caronni is in itself an intriguing account of travel, piracy and archaeology in the Napoleonic era. He writes about embarking on a Sicilian ship in Palermo harbour bound for Napoli with oranges to sell. Thirty miles south of Capri another ship appeared, coming out of the port of Salerno as the sun was rising. The captain and sixteen of the crew fled the ship in the only lifeboat, leaving the passengers alone to face the pirates. The result was that Father Caronni was deposited along with the other passengers in Tunis. There he found himself needing a new passport that proved his Milanese credentials. This was key because of Milan's role in the short-lived Italian Republic of 1802–5 which was allied with Napoleonic France. France had a treaty with the bey at Tunis which meant that, in theory, its citizens should not be captured by pirates and sold into slavery for ransom. It was a complex moment in Mediterranean and European history. Caronni navigated this complexity by replacing his passport and proving his citizenship, which would lead to his being freed.

By coincidence, the priest from Milan also happened to be a keen classicist and amateur antiquarian. When Caronni found himself so close to the great ancient site of Carthage, he was intrigued. At the suggestion of the French consul in Tunis, Caronni went to stay at the Danish consul's residence, which was located at La Marsa, an area that would once have been part of ancient Carthage (see Map 1.2 in Chapter 1). For three weeks, sometimes on foot and sometimes on horseback, he diverted himself among the ruins of the ancient city under the expert guidance of none other than Jean Emile Humbert. Immediately upon his return to Italy in 1805, Caronni published his observations to great success.[11] Perhaps the most significant aspect of the work was that the correct location of the Punic ports had been noted for the first time. It seems unlikely that this was Caronni's own observation, for the sketched map included in his publication seems to be based on Humbert's ideas on the topography of the city (see Figure 3.2). So it is to Humbert that this important discovery must be attributed.

Tunis and Carthage were becoming popular destinations to visit and two influential characters followed shortly after Caronni. The priest's publication is mentioned by Chateaubriand in the account of his pilgrimage to ancient sites in 1806 and 1807. Although Chateaubriand claims that he was unable to acquire a copy of Caronni's work before he left on his journey, he was certainly familiar with it. Chateaubriand spent six weeks in the area around

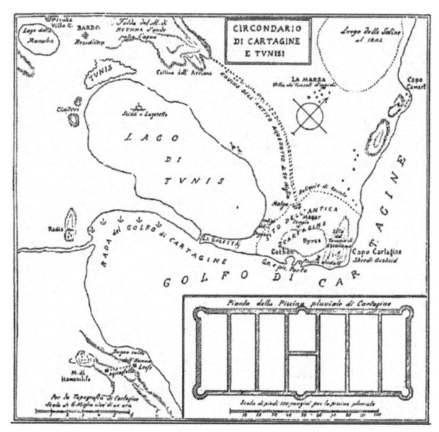

FIGURE 3.2 *Sketch plans of the Punic ports by Father Caronni (Caronni, 1805).*

Carthage in early 1807, coming into contact with Humbert, who showed him around the site. Chateaubriand also engaged with the question of the location of the ports, agreeing that Humbert – and therefore, Caronni – had identified the location correctly. His published acceptance of the location helped to disseminate more widely an understanding of the site topography in the early part of the nineteenth century. But perhaps the most significant visitor of the Napoleonic era to have contact with Humbert at Carthage was Camillo Borgia, who arrived in Tunis in 1815.[12] Borgia, an educated Italian nobleman from Velletri, was a soldier and proto-archaeologist of note. He had led a colourful life during the Napoleonic period as chamberlain to Napoleon's flamboyant cavalry marshal, Joachim Murat. Murat himself, King of Naples from 1808 to 1815, along with his wife Caroline Bonaparte (Napoleon's sister), was an influential and enthusiastic supporter of excavations at Pompeii during his short reign. Borgia was then familiar with the work going on at Pompeii and had spent a good deal of time there. In 1815, when Murat had made his wayward attempt at Italian unification,

Borgia had marched north with an army to meet him. After being soundly defeated by the Austrians at the Battle of Tolentino, near Ancona, Murat was forced to abandon his Neapolitan kingdom and Borgia was sent into exile in Tunis.

Fresh from the Pompeii excavations which had thrilled the public – and with not much else to do – Borgia immediately teamed up with Humbert and turned his interest to Carthage and to the other archaeological remains of Tunisia. With a noble pedigree, Borgia had full access to the bey and his ministers, who granted him the right to excavate and to measure for topographical information. He was active both further north at the site of Utica (see Map 1.2 in Chapter 1) and with Humbert at Carthage. Up until this point, the antiquities that had originated at Carthage – all sculpture, coins and inscriptions – were almost entirely without provenance. Most were sold to collectors by whoever found them, ranging from ministers of the government to passers-by and local inhabitants. Although Borgia spent only one year in Tunis (1815–16), his interests seem to have convinced Mahmoud Bey (ruled 1814–24), who had only just assumed power, to allow wider archaeological exploration in his kingdom. This was a major breakthrough for those interested in pursuing further research at Carthage. The previous ruler of the kingdom of Tunis, Hammouda Bey, had been largely unwilling to grant permission for excavations, but his successor was more open to archaeologists and exploration at the site. The reluctance of the authorities in Tunis was based on a variety of geopolitical considerations. In particular, a fear of espionage and possible preparation for invasion had restricted any active surveying and map-making. Humbert noted exactly this in a letter that outlined how suspicion of archaeological research lessened to some degree after 1816. The change in policy seems to have been a result of both the personal interaction of Borgia with the bey and the wider political impact of the defeat of Napoleon. A significant act by the British Navy, which bombed Algiers during the 'Battle of Algiers' on 27 August 1816, effectively brought an end to piracy in the Mediterranean.[13] A combination of all these events left the cities and hinterland of North Africa opened to wider exploration.

Humbert acted as host and guided celebrity visitors around the site while still involved in ongoing research and excavations too. From his records we know that between 1822 and 1824, Humbert carried out six separate excavations that lasted a total of thirty-seven days. His excellent relationship with the bey gave him unparalleled access to sites around Carthage and across Tunisia as well. Humbert should be acknowledged as the very first 'real' archaeologist at Carthage and it is much to his credit that his finds and their location are almost all recorded. Notable among them is the find-spot of a Punic stele and other fragments that are significant because they are the first recorded Punic remains in situ to come to light at Carthage (see Figure 3.3). Humbert found the Punic material on 6 January 1817 but intriguingly did not make it publicly known until 1821 when he published

FIGURE 3.3 *The first published sketch of stelae from Carthage (Wikipedia).*

his finds as the first proof of the topography of the Punic city. The gap in time between discovery and publication reveals a reluctance to disclose information about the site. During this period of the late 1810s and early 1820s, there was an atmosphere of secrecy and rivalry among those working at Carthage. There was also an aspect of national interest in archaeological excavations that reflected the broader impact of cultural artefacts and heritage at play in the geopolitical ambitions of European nations.

In the early nineteenth century at Carthage this is best exemplified by Humbert. His work was closely followed and supported by C. J. C. Reuvens, the director of the Dutch Archaeological Museum, who saw research at Carthage as a way for the Dutch to make their name in the competitive world of collection and acquisition of antiquities. The work of Jean Emile Humbert at the site of Carthage superseded all other aspects of his life. The ancient city was a constant and when he died in 1839, part of his epitaph read, 'Who was useful to the sciences / By his discoveries on the ruins of Carthage.' Fortunately, Humbert's notebooks and many reference papers survived and his collections form the basis for the National Museum of Antiquities at Leiden, with modern scholars noting his influence on the early archaeological research at the site. Humbert is justly credited as the 'founder of systematic archaeological research' at Carthage.[14]

The next steps towards an understanding of the topography of the ancient city of Carthage were taken by the Danish consul general, Christian Tuxen Falbe. Falbe arrived in Tunis as acting consul for the Crown Prince of

Denmark in 1821 and remained there through to 1832. He was a naval captain and skilled cartographer, with a keen interest in archaeology and antiquities. Falbe's contribution, built on the foundation of Humbert's research, was to produce a comprehensive archaeological reference map of the site and the surrounding area. It was a major achievement and in 1833, he published his work entitled *Research on the Location of Carthage*. Falbe was on a mission to gather factual information on the city of Carthage that was 'so little known despite its ancient fame', as he wrote in a letter to the king of France (to whom the book is dedicated). Falbe's meticulous quantification of the various sites of interest set out to establish once and for all the actual and precise location of the ancient city. He intended to create a base from which other research could be conducted. Falbe went about his work with a copy of Appian's famous topographical description of the ancient city of Punic Carthage in hand. Over a period of two years, Falbe walked the site, measuring and noting every bit of masonry and rubble he came across, from Lac Tunis in the south to Cap Gammarth in the north (see Map 1.2 in Chapter 1).

The quantification of the visible ruins at Carthage in these years was not a simple task of taking measurements. Falbe presents his research and exploration at the site as taking place quietly, without arousing the suspicions of the government. He refers to the authorities as 'envious and troubled', implying that the rulers in Tunis did not support *his* research but did allow others to work at the site. The background to this may well lie in the French occupation of Algeria that had just taken place in 1830. The subsequent engagement concerning borders saw Constantine (now in modern Algeria) claimed for Tunisia by the Ottomans. The Ottomans were, at the time, fighting an independence movement in their prized province of Greece (1821–32). It was a dangerous period for the leadership in Tunis and for the Ottoman power in Istanbul, with the natural result being that Europeans working at Carthage were now held in more suspicion than in the previous decade. Yet even without official support, Falbe succeeded beyond what he could ever have imagined in his creation of a map of Carthage. His map is still in use today and places of note and references around the site are referred to as 'Falbe Points'. By describing and mapping what was there, on the ground, in the 1820s and early 1830s, Falbe achieved a kind of archaeological immortality at Carthage (see Figure 3.4).[15]

One aspect of the work at Carthage that Falbe described during his time as consul at Tunis was an atmosphere of factional rivalry between nationalities. In one anecdote, he writes of the discovery of a large mosaic (30-foot square) close to the sea located at point ninety on his map.[16] He then claims that three days after the discovery, the Maritime Minister of the bey arrived with some men to dig up the mosaic at the instigation of 'an unnamed European antiquarian'. This unnamed adversary seems to have convinced the minister that a lead case full of gold and silver coins would be found under the mosaic. Falbe rails a bit at the 'antiquarian' who he claims

FIGURE 3.4 *Falbe map (Alamy).*

wanted to reserve the right to all that was found at Carthage for himself, and adds, with a classic academic dig, that the finds of this antiquarian had yet to be published. It seems possible, although it is nowhere stated, that Falbe is referring to the Dutch engineer Humbert, who never finished his master manuscript on the ancient site. It would be Falbe who had the last word, for, with the publication of his map, he rendered much of the unpublished work of Humbert out of date.

If Falbe had succeeded in setting out and quantifying what was on the ground, it is the extravagantly named Adolphe Jules César Auguste Dureau de la Malle (1777–1857) who recorded what should have been there, according to the ancient sources. Dureau de la Malle also offered an idea of what he suspected might still be lurking under the ground. Even though he had never visited the site, in 1835 Dureau de la Malle published a study on the topography of Carthage.[17] He wrote extensively and creatively about the minute details of life at Carthage in both the Punic and Roman periods, and was also quite frank about the lack of answers to the questions presented in the sources relating to the content and location of much of Punic and Roman Carthage. Dureau de la Malle, with his copy of Falbe's map, was concerned with the issues that were occupying the mind of the antiquarian at this time in relation to Carthage. His work is half taken up by musing on the exact location of many of the urban characteristics that the ancient sources claim made up Punic Carthage. His sources vary from Virgil and Appian to Orosius and Polybius, Strabo and Procopius. His textual research, like others before him, was extensive and thorough and, by following the ancient sources, he claimed to be able to prove the exact location of the different camps from which the Romans led their attacks on Carthage in 146 BCE.

Other sites of specific interest that are mentioned by Dureau de la Malle include the location of the Temple of Juno (Astarte) discussed in Virgil, the location of the ports, the Byrsa hill, and even the palace of the legendary Dido. While remaining conscious of how little evidence other than textual existed at this time, Dureau de la Malle's imagination was at work as much as his knowledge, especially when it came to the early Punic period at Carthage. On Roman Carthage he had more to work with. He considers the source of the aqueduct and the reoccupation of the city in the first century BCE. It is worth noting that many of the issues that occupied Dureau de la Malle still concern archaeologists at the site of Carthage today.

Dureau de la Malle was a key player in the foundation of a society that had in mind the financing of further investigation at the site. The Society for the Exploration of Carthage came into being in 1838 and included among its founding members Christian Falbe and Major Sir Grenville Temple, author of *Excursions in the Mediterranean, Algiers and Tunis* (published in 1835). The intent of the Society was, as stated in Article 1 of the Acts, 'to execute excavations of Carthage, based on the Falbe plan, and to export to France objects of art and science that they find'. The members had high expectations for future archaeological glory and increased wealth as Dureau de la Malle noted in an article in which he compared the potential of Carthage with what had already happened in Italy:

If digs executed on the antique soil of a few obscure towns in Italy have produced such important results (Volterra, Ruvo, Napoli etc.), just imagine what awaits when similar work will take place with enterprise and intelligence on a soil still untouched of such a celebrated capital, so opulent and sumptuously decorated as ancient Carthage.

The plan, then, was that the members – eighteen in number, by invitation only – would provide the funds in exchange for the finds. Here was focused plunder at the site on a new level. With so little left above ground, what was beneath the surface was to be uncovered and exported. The governing bey was on-board and permission to both excavate and export materials gave the founding members of the Society a footing from which to set off to explore future potential.

The first results of the joint efforts of Christian Falbe and Grenville Temple were published in 1838. The fate of one mosaic pavement is enough to exemplify what happened to artefacts that were excavated during the reign of the Society over archaeology at Carthage. A large marine mosaic from the late antique period was lifted from near the sea and cut up. The largest part went to the British Museum and another part was poorly restored and wound up in the library at Versailles. Thirty-one crates of the mosaic were sent to various localities, including Toulon, Marseille and Le Havre. The pieces excavated were sold, with profits being partially channelled back into the Society to fund further research. The Society for the Exploration of Carthage typifies the way that Carthage was both a goal and a quest for many European explorers hoping to make their names in the race for antiquities.

The post-antique period at Carthage had seen the site mused over by early Islamic scholars, exploited for the valuable building stone and explored for remnants of its epic past to be sold to European museums. Along with all this, there was much conjuring of the idea of the ancient city in the popular imagination. There was a paradoxical approach to the archaeology at Carthage, and the disappointment of the early archaeologists did not deter visitors from all over Europe who turned up to ponder the historical lessons that Carthage offered.[18] If these visitors were inspired and well connected enough, they also had the opportunity to poke around in the ground. The English consul to Tunis in the mid-nineteenth century, Thomas Reade (consul from 1824 to 1849), is a perfect example of one such amateur and collector involved in both politics and archaeology at Carthage. Reade had once served as Napoleon's jailor on St Helena and is perhaps better known for collecting manuscripts than artefacts, but he nonetheless had an impact at the ancient site. Reade was close to the new ruler, Ahmed Bey (ruled 1837–55), who saw himself as a modernizer. Among his most notable acts was the abolition of slavery in Tunisia in 1846. The bey was broadly encouraging to archaeological and scientific research at Carthage and this allowed diplomats like Reade to excavate without much hindrance. That was how Reade found himself working at one of the most visibly recognizable parts of ancient Carthage, the great Roman imperial baths built at the seaside (see Figure 1.3 in Chapter 1). In the early nineteenth century, Reade excavated at the site at his own expense and the British Museum received any moveable artefacts he discovered. The current catalogue at the British Museum lists 315 artefacts. The complex was eventually identified as having been built by the second-century Antonine emperors through an inscription discovered decades later.[19]

The study of Carthage had now been transformed from an endeavour that relied almost exclusively on textual analysis to the beginnings of practical archaeological research on the ground. One often relied on the other and interpretation was based on the search for a Carthage as described by the writing of ancient authors. The continued narrative and stories of dismay at the state of the ruins prevailed among the Europeans at the site and would play an important part when European countries developed a colonial interest in North Africa. The narrative that combines a continual European disappointment with what could be seen at Carthage and continued interest in archaeological exploration plays into the idea of the wrack and ruin that had arrived in North Africa after the abandonment of the region by the 'classical' world. We can return to the latent Orientalist ideas in Chateaubriand's description of Tunis and Carthage that outlines this dichotomy: Tunis is the decadent and Carthage the glorious – even while he laments the state of the ruins.

This narrative would be picked up and exploited once the colonial occupation of the countries of North Africa took hold and would be the means by which the European inhabitants would separate the autochthonous and Arab populations from their history and archaeology. The European claims of bringing civilization and Christianity anew in the nineteenth century were built upon this repeated and oft cited description of the region and all its glory gone to ruin. The idea of equating European and Roman conquests was not unique to the period and we have already seen that the Holy Roman Emperor Charles V did just that in his own battles over Tunis. However, in the nineteenth and early twentieth centuries, the narrative of conquest and Roman civilization would again be used by the colonial occupiers to justify their actions and would result in a long period of disenfranchisement of the local population from their history and archaeology.[20]

4

Rivals in the Field

In March 1859, the *Illustrated London News* carried a notice about work being done at Carthage:

> The excavations on the site of ancient Carthage, now in course of being carried on with so much success, have naturally attracted the attention of the civilized world, and literary, scientific, and fashionable tourists now bend their course to the Tunisian shore. A few years ago, says a letter just received from Tunis, the European traveller seldom approached this coast; but, during the period that some of the remains of the once mighty metropolis of Africa are being exhumed, every steamer brings fresh visitors to this scene. The spade and the pickaxe daily demonstrate the fallacy of the hitherto universally entertained opinion that the very ruins of Carthage had perished.[1]

That Carthage had not perished was becoming more and more apparent in the mid to late nineteenth century, with the work of Falbe, Dureau de la Malle and Grenville Temple providing the foundation upon which others could build. Although there was still not all that much to see on the ground, the lure of a site with such a rich history was clearly tempting for many, with new finds emerging all the time.

Among those active in archaeological exploration at Carthage in the mid-nineteenth century, two key individuals – and their personal and professional rivalry – stand out. The Reverend Nathan Davis (1812–82) was an English Anglican missionary; and Charles-Ernest Beulé (1826–74), an experienced excavator and French academic. History has been less kind to Davis, not without reason, but that both men had a pivotal role to play in the further discovery of the site cannot be denied. They could not have been more different in their approaches and at times their relationship was antagonistic. This is perhaps less surprising when one considers the broader context in which they were working, namely the British–French geopolitical rivalry in Tunisia in this period (1856–9).[2] Both powers were eager to maintain influence in the country, though France had the more pressing concerns, focused on the need to ensure the security of the border between Algeria and

Tunisia. In 1855, the death of Ahmed Bey saw his cousin, Mohammed Bey, come to power. In that same year, new diplomatic consuls were officially appointed by France and Great Britain. The two diplomats, Léon Roches and Richard Wood, occasionally found common cause in their dealings with Mohammed Bey, but were all too ready to undermine one another. France had the upper hand from the start, mainly because it was in the interests of both the bey and the French government that they cooperate. The bey needed to ensure that Tunisia retained the measure of independence from the Ottoman Empire that his predecessors had enjoyed and France was intent on keeping the border with Algeria secure. The British for their part did not give up trying to gain an advantage, in particular by proposing infrastructure projects, but without much success since they were blocked by the French at every opportunity. This, then, was the atmosphere in which Davis and Beulé were excavating at Carthage.

Nathan Davis had already spent time in North Africa before discovering an interest in archaeology.[3] In 1841, he published a book titled *Tunis: or Selections from a Journal during a Residence in that Regency*, which shows that he had been in the country for some time before he undertook excavations. His long tenure in the area and fluency in Arabic were valuable in his new pursuit. Even more importantly, he was on friendly terms with Mohammed Bey. Their relationship had been forged when the bey was still heir to the throne. Davis had been part of the bey's entourage during a tour of the Regency some years before (the term Regency refers to the *beylic* of Tunis from 1705 to 1881). His record of this trip was published as *Evenings in my Tent* in 1854. It did not take long for Davis to ingratiate himself with the court once Mohammed Bey came to power, even though they had not been in touch for some time. It was through this personal relationship, and with the support of the British consul Richard Wood, that Davis was granted permission to excavate in Carthage where, as we have seen, the beys were not always that willing to allow or support excavation. With official permission from the Tunisian government, Davis was also able to gain support from the British Museum and the Foreign Office, illustrating the way that archaeology, politics and diplomacy interacted in this crucial period.

In considering Davis' contribution to the understanding of the site, we are hampered by the nature of the publication he produced. The title, *Carthage and her Remains: being an Account of the Excavations and Researches on the Site of the Phoenician Metropolis in Africa, and other Adjacent Places*, sums up a work that is more a narration of his experiences than a report of his excavations. Davis noted in the introduction that the reader of his day wanted knowledge and information to be concise but also to be conveyed in 'an attractive and fascinating manner'.[4] So, he says, 'he sought to combine his special object – to dig for relics of the past, with his natural propensity to dig into the minds, and characters, of the modern occupants of the territories of Carthage'.[5] The resulting volume is an eclectic assortment of information, ranging from conversations Davis had in the souk in Tunis to discussion concerning the ports of Carthage. Along the way, there are chapters on the history of Carthage, on the religion of the city, on the area around Carthage and, occasionally, on the excavations themselves. One critic in the early twentieth century, Auguste Audollent, noted that the immediate impression is favourable, given the size of the book, but that one soon realizes that it does not live up to expectations, with far too many tedious anecdotes about Davis' workmen or stories of Arab legends.[6] So while the work met the remit of Davis' time in being 'attractive and fascinating', it tells the reader little overall about the results of his excavations or methodology.

Yet the motives for including some of the information is easily understood. Davis had played tour guide to some well-known individuals and he was not going to miss the opportunity to boast of that fact. Two in particular are of note. Lady Jane Franklin, widow of the celebrated Arctic explorer John Franklin, along with her niece Sophia Cracroft arrived in the spring of 1858 having undertaken the journey for health reasons. Davis mentions that her visit was 'to divert her mind from the one preponderating idea – the fate of Sir John and his companions. The classic shores of Carthage and Utica proved sufficiently attractive to her; and her visits to these localities will ever be remembered by African friends with the utmost pleasure.'[7] In a letter of 26 May 1858, sent from Malta, Sophia recounts their recent visit to Carthage with Davis as their guide, noting that evidence of the once great city – columns, mosaics, remains of temples, cisterns – were dotted about the site, along with signs of other, still buried, ruins.[8] As many before them, Lady Franklin and her niece were captivated by the prospect of what excavation had already uncovered and might reveal in the future, even on such a short visit. Carthage clearly had become a destination for fashionable Europeans and British to show off their intellectual aspirations. Davis also provides a detailed description of a visit to the site made by Prince Alfred, second son of Queen Victoria, in January of 1859. He was asked to accompany the young prince on a tour of Carthage, a singular honour. Whether the prince was there only to see the ruins or to test the attitude of the bey towards Britain is not entirely clear. Davis indicated that the bey had 'at all times entertained most friendly feelings towards Great Britain' and was 'resolved to embrace this opportunity to demonstrate his partiality'.[9] Yet in *The Times* of 25 January 1859, any political intent was downplayed: 'His Royal Highness had requested Mr Davis, now excavating on the site of Carthage, to attend him [the day after his arrival]. It was at once seen that there was no political question connected with the Prince's visit, but that this classic land was his only attention.' It must be said that it is often difficult to distinguish genuine interest in antiquity from political expediency, especially in the nineteenth century when archaeology, heritage, celebrity and politics all coalesced.

To be fair to Davis with respect to *Carthage and her Remains*, it should be noted that he did make it clear at the outset that the current work was not to be his final word. He claimed that he intended to publish an account of the excavations that would include finds as well as plans, all 'embellished by upwards of one hundred illustrations, executed in the best style'.[10] In fact, he had been encouraged to produce such an account by several individuals, including the curator at the British Museum, Augustus Franks. Since most of Davis' finds were destined for that museum, such a report would have provided useful information for those who wished to study them. 'I trust that Mr Davis may be induced to publish a minute account of his excavations,' Franks wrote in the journal *Archaeologia* in 1860, 'as by so doing he will add greatly to the value of his researches.'[11] That final report never appeared.

Gaining funding for excavations in this early period of archaeology at Carthage proved challenging for Davis. He had thought at first of putting together a society that would provide the necessary financing, in emulation of the French Society for the Exploration of Carthage. He was supported in this idea by several distinguished names in British archaeology. Davis mentions Sir John Gardiner Wilkinson, the renowned Egyptologist who had mapped the Valley of the Kings in 1827, and Sir Austen Henry Layard, the British archaeologist who had excavated Nineveh and Nimrud between 1839 and 1850. But since Davis realized that any finds would be distributed among the society members or auctioned off to the highest bidder, thus making them inaccessible to the wider public, he decided instead to offer the artefacts from his excavations to the British Museum. The decision meant that the enrichment of the museum became his sole focus at the expense of more 'scientific' excavation. As noted earlier, there was initial support at the museum for Davis in his endeavours: ancient Carthage was fashionable with the public and Antonio Panizzi, the Principal Librarian of the British Museum, hoped to secure Punic material for the collection. It should be said, however, that they were not footing the bill. Davis' funding came from the Foreign Office, an element of his story which Joanne Freed in her book on Davis has observed was quite unusual.[12] There was undoubtedly a political element at play here, given the geopolitical climate, but it was all kept rather quiet. Davis himself notes in passing that 'from the commencement of the excavations it has been my aim to work in such a manner as not to attract public attention, and particularly the attention of Europeans'.[13] It is clear that archaeological pursuits were not just for the purposes of revealing more about ancient Carthage, but in fact, discovery and acquisition were in themselves powerful incentives in the ongoing rivalry between the British and the French.

Davis excavated in Carthage for just over two years, between November 1856 and March 1859. The work was carried out piecemeal and the chronology of his excavations is difficult to determine. Davis himself refers to his endeavours as 'migratory excavating operations'.[14] In the early stages, he consulted the plans of his predecessors, especially that of Falbe, but to no avail. And so, like others before him, he decided to rely instead on ancient authorities. He indicates in his chapter on the ports that he made use of Polybius, Sallust, Livy, Strabo and Appian, although he also confessed to be relying on 'common sense'.[15] Fanciful ideas of the Punic city certainly influenced his intentions. In fact, his work is characterized by a credulity that seems incomprehensible to the modern reader. For example, he argued strenuously that Virgil's story of Dido in the *Aeneid* was based on historical fact and that one could use the poem, therefore, to gain an appreciation of what Carthage was like during her reign. His discussion of the so-called Temple of Ba'al provides another example of his active imagination. In chapter thirteen of *Carthage and her Remains*, Davis notes how he came to excavate at a site already examined by Grenville Temple and Falbe, where he was certain he would discover the temple. He argued that the earlier excavators had not gone deep enough. What could be seen above ground was a circular structure with pilasters and arches. When he dug down in the middle of the building, Davis came upon burnt earth mixed with bones lying upon natural rock. He could not resist concluding that he had discovered the very place where children had been sacrificed to the god: 'As for the centre, I am satisfied in my own mind that here stood the brazen image of the terrible Baal [*sic*], which Diodorus of Sicily describes as having had outstretched arms, inclined to the earth, so that the child that was placed on them rolled down and fell into a pit below, filled with fire.'[16] So consumed by his imagination and the ancient sources was Davis that when he came upon a layer of burning in situ, possibly related to the Roman destruction of the city, he insisted it was 'ashes and bones . . . and therefore the remains of the victims immolated to this divinity'.[17]

Like many of his predecessors, Davis had decided to focus on the Punic city to the exclusion of all else. He joined in the pastime of Carthaginian topography, in particular the placement of the ports, but added little to the knowledge already circulating. In fact, his topographic plan has several errors. Most notable is his placement of the Byrsa hill (see Plan 1.1 in Chapter 1) as a separate entity from what he refers to as the Hill of St Louis. Davis provides a robust defence of his view in a chapter entitled 'Disputed Topography – Temple of Aesculapius', in which he challenges all those who had argued that the two were the same. This challenge was aimed not only at Falbe but also Davis' great rival Beulé.

Davis was blinded by a belief that whatever he exposed must be Punic, even when it was clear that it was not. Perhaps the best example is that of a mosaic he uncovered, now in the British Museum, which he associated with a chapel belonging to the precinct of what he believed to be the Temple of Astarte. The female figures depicted in the main body of the mosaic were identified by Davis as priestesses (see Figure 4.1; the colour plates in *Carthage and her Remains*, produced while the mosaic was still in situ, show the full splendour of the decoration). Key to his interpretation were large female heads in the two extant corners of the mosaic. These, he argued, represented Dido (or her sister Anna) and the goddess Ceres, with the missing figures then

FIGURE 4.1 *Mosaic showing one of the seasons (© The Trustees of the British Museum).*

corresponding to Anna (or perhaps Dido) and Proserpina, the daughter of Ceres. The mosaic is clearly Roman but Davis persisted in erroneously referring to it as Punic: 'From what has already been stated it is clear that I ascribe to these mosaics a remote, or Punic, antiquity, and in doing this I am aware that contrary opinions have already been advanced . . .'[18] He then goes on – for nearly twenty pages – to refute any interpretation that suggested otherwise. First among these individuals was Beulé, whom he decries as only 'professing . . . to be an archaeologist'.[19] Yet, despite Davis' view, the British Museum was clear in its identification of the mosaic as Roman:

> We must not omit to notice the valuable collection of mosaics from Carthage, recently excavated and sent home by the Rev. Nathan Davis. They belong to the Roman period. Two exquisite full-length female figures – one of a dancing girl, the other in a careless and graceful attitude

of repose, in a standing posture and holding the spray of a flower in her hand – deserve the highest encomium that can be bestowed upon them.[20]

It is clear that Davis was willing to tie himself in knots trying to justify and convince the world that he alone had discovered the secrets to Punic Carthage.

At times Davis did not care about what was destroyed in the process of exposing these finds. In this regard, he was acting in a similar fashion to many other nineteenth-century archaeologists. Throughout *Carthage and her Remains*, any period other than Punic – be it Roman, Christian or Vandal – is of little if any interest to the excavator. In fact, at one point, he uncovered a wall imbedded with Punic inscriptions. Davis' account will strike fear into the heart of the modern archaeologist:

> As we were determined to secure every trophy, we were absolutely compelled to demolish the walls in which they were imbedded. This process of destruction, under other circumstances perfectly inexcusable, prevented us from ascertaining the real nature of the building itself. That it was Roman, there could be no doubt; and that it was a structure of some importance, its extent, and the massiveness of its walls, amply proved; but whether it was a Roman temple, a palace, or a sumptuous edifice of a private citizen, will, in all probability, after the havoc we were under the necessity to cause, never be ascertained.[21]

Though Davis himself admits that such destruction would normally be unacceptable, he nonetheless considered that the stelae were worth the price of destruction. Like many others, Davis never seems to consider recording the building before demolition. It is expected that the British Museum was pleased to receive these Punic inscriptions, considering both their rarity and that the main reason for supporting him was to acquire such artefacts. A *Daily News* article of 5 October 1859 mentions their significance: 'Besides the mosaics, Mr Davis has sent home a number of fragments of statuary, etc., of rude workmanship, but many of them most valuable in a philological point of view, as containing Phenician [*sic*] inscriptions.' Davis' own interpretations of these stelae were far-fetched, based on a rudimentary reading of the texts and on an attempt to connect them with the ancient sources. In *Carthage and her Remains* he devotes an entire chapter to 'The Religion of the Carthaginians', in which these stones are discussed. The stelae themselves ended up in the British Museum, and a more scholarly study of them was produced by W. S. W. Vaux in 1863. A recent examination of Punic stelae in the museum by Carolyn Mendleson has shown that Davis sent back approximately 100 of them (see Figure 4.2).[22]

Davis' most significant contribution to archaeology at Carthage relates to the methodology of mosaic removal.[23] Despite the lack of visible remains of the ancient city, he found thirty-one mosaics in total, some with figures and

FIGURE 4.2 *Limestone stele with a dedication to Ba'al excavated by Nathan Davis (© The Trustees of the British Museum).*

some geometric, which was a feat in itself.[24] At the time, the usual method for taking up mosaics was to strengthen them by adding layers (made of canvas and plaster of Paris) to fix the tesserae. The mosaic was then removed by digging around and underneath it. This rather crude method often resulted in destruction and also meant that only small pieces could be lifted. Davis came up with an ingenious new method to lift the in-situ mosaics. He describes how they would first use carpenters' glue to attach canvas to the surface of the mosaic, leaving it to set. The next step separated the mosaic from the ancient cement and a board was placed on top and nailed to one edge of the canvas. By carefully flipping it over, any remaining ancient cement was removed and the mosaic was placed in a specially prepared case where new cement was poured in and another board screwed on. Once the new cement had set, they unscrewed the first board and removed the canvas, by softening the glue with water. As Davis himself says, 'The mosaic was now again before us in all its freshness and beauty; indeed, by this process of removal many of its imperfections were rectified.'[25] He could now divide the mosaics into manageable sizes and, with due care, preserve the designs or figures. The mosaics Davis excavated all arrived at the British Museum intact.

Davis' exploration of Carthage was finally brought to a halt by those who had initially been supportive. The British Museum was concerned both about the lack of Punic material and about the costs to the government. Changes at the Foreign Office also served to complicate things. The Earl of Clarendon, Secretary of State for Foreign Affairs, to whom *Carthage and her Remains* is dedicated, stepped down in the spring of 1858 and his successors were less supportive of the eccentric Davis. The lines of communication between Davis, the British Museum and the Foreign Office were fractured. In her book on Davis, Joanne Freed provides details about correspondence between Carthage and London that reveals the gradual withdrawal of support.[26] In January 1859, Davis was asked to finish excavating, but he ignored the directives for several months, only stopping in October of that year when it was clear that funding truly had come to an end. Moreover, the death of Mohammed Bey that autumn meant that Davis could no longer rely on support from the local authorities. It is likely, though, that the long delay in wrapping up his work must also reflect Davis' reluctance to leave while his great rival, Charles-Ernest Beulé, was still excavating.[27] The contrast between the two men could not have been greater. As a professor at the École Française in Athens, Beulé had participated in excavations on the Acropolis (1852–3), where he discovered the so-called Beulé Gate, the late Roman entrance west of the Propylaia. He was given many honours on his return to Paris, including an appointment as Professor of Archaeology at the Bibliothèque Imperiale, a position which he held until his death. Before working at Carthage, Beulé had published extensively on a wide range of topics including art history and numismatics, in particular on Athenian coins. When he decided to return to the field, he chose Carthage as his destination because of a trip he had taken to Selinunte in Sicily in 1851. The evocative ruins there had sparked his interest in the culture and city of Carthage.

Beulé also considered that his work would be in the national interest. In the context of the British–French geopolitical rivalry, he argued that the French should excavate in Carthage because the British were already doing so. It would be eight years before Beulé could get to the site, however, and it may have been at the behest of the French consul in Tunis, Léon Roches, that he was given the opportunity to excavate at all. Roches is mentioned several times in Beulé's letters, always with great gratitude. This was partly because the consul had granted Beulé the use of his villa near Carthage as his base of operations while excavating and also because Roches was a keen supporter of the operation. It is clear from the outset that both men regarded the French–British rivalry a key motivation for the archaeological work. In fact, there is much condemnation of the British in Beulé's correspondence, in particular, relating to the enrichment of the British Museum and the lack of publication of excavation results. Though these criticisms are included in his discussion of other important sites in the Mediterranean, it is hard not to read in this correspondence a denunciation of Davis' activity at Carthage.

Beulé's excavations in Carthage occurred within a very compressed time frame. He worked for one month in February 1859 and then later that same year from October to December. The results of these excavations were published in 1861 in a book titled *Fouilles à Carthage aux frais et sous la direction de M. Beulé* (Excavations at Carthage at the expense and under the direction of M. Beulé). In this work, he provides a thorough account of what he did in the field as well as background information on the sites. The book is divided into three parts. The first section, by far the longest in the book, offers an historical overview of the Byrsa hill, as well as comments on those who had visited the site in the past, including Shaw, Caroni and Falbe. Beulé was not afraid here to correct earlier impressions where needed, which allows his work to be placed in the broader context of early archaeology at Carthage. The second part of the book discusses the ports, again with historical background. For the final section on the necropolis at Gammarth (see Map 1.2 in Chapter 1), Beulé includes comparanda for the tombs he investigated. Correspondence written at Carthage during the excavation period was then published several years later in 1873. This volume contains four letters on Carthage itself, each dealing with a single aspect of the site: the Byrsa hill, the aqueduct, the necropolis at Gammarth and finally the ports. Addressed to members of the Académie des Inscriptions et Belles-Lettres in Paris (Academy of Inscriptions and Belles-Lettres, hereafter referred to as the Academy), they reveal that Beulé saw the need to get preliminary reports to France as quickly as possible, though he did not decide to publish the letters as a collection for many years. In the first letter from Carthage, dated 19 March 1859, Beulé acknowledges what both the Society for the Exploration of Carthage and Nathan Davis had accomplished there. He emphatically makes the point that he is interested only in the architecture of the site, not in enriching museums. Like those before him, Beulé was captivated by the Punic city. In his first excavation, he concentrated on the Byrsa hill for two reasons. First, he did not need permission to excavate there: land on the Byrsa hill had been gifted to the French in 1830 by the bey for the construction of a small chapel to Saint Louis (dedicated in 1841). Second, he reasoned that the Romans could not have destroyed every trace on the hill of what must have been sizeable Punic structures: in particular, he expected to find architectural remains of the fortifications. Beulé professed not to be interested in terracottas and mosaics, perhaps a direct taunt at Davis. Rather, it was architecture that he was after, and, as he remarked in his monograph, he felt that if he found even a single stone from the 'old' – that is, Punic – city, he would enrich science and fill an archaeological gap.[28]

Because of his circumstances, in particular a lack of time and of suitable equipment, Beulé could only examine a small area on the southeast of the Byrsa hill. He used test pits, rather than the huge trenches typical of the era, to achieve his goals. Beulé's work on the hill revealed much Roman material, walls and cisterns in particular (see Figure 4.3). What he argued were Punic walls (marked at 'G' on his plan) were in fact Roman. These walls formed part of the retaining wall constructed when the Byrsa hill was levelled in the early first century CE, as was proven over a century later by the French excavations

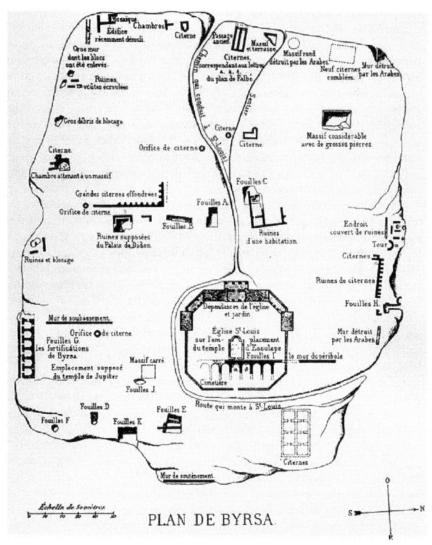

PLAN DE BYRSA.

FIGURE 4.3 *Plan of the Byrsa by Beulé (Charles-Ernest Beulé, 1861).*

in the 1970s. One other discovery of significance came about through an examination of the area around the Chapel of Saint Louis ('I' on the plan). Fragments of architectural decoration found in close proximity to this building resembled those exposed during its construction. In this area, Beulé uncovered several apses, forming part of what he interpreted to be the palace of the pro-consul due to the quality of the decoration within the main apse. In fact, later excavations showed this to be the vaulted platform of a second-century CE Roman basilica. Before Beulé had a chance to explore the area fully, however, he had to return to Paris. Previous commitments as well as the need to avoid the heat of the summer are given as the reasons – but since he was self-financing his work, the cost may also have been of consideration.

On his second trip to Carthage, in the autumn of 1859, Beulé gained a strategic advantage since Davis was being forced to abandon his excavations. Because Beulé was irritated by the lack of support from the French government for his project, he decided to cease work on the Byrsa hill. Instead, he chose to investigate the necropolis at Gammarth, just outside Carthage, in an attempt to ascertain the architecture of the tombs. The third letter in his collection gives a brief overview of the excavations here (the fuller report appears in *Fouilles à Carthage*). Dated to mid-November 1859, it reveals how quickly he had managed to accomplish these investigations. Beulé indicates that he had examined several of the tombs and excavated a few, despite the difficulty of working underground. An account of his methodology – determining where in the hill there were voids and then removing the topsoil over a wide area to find a way in – is given in some detail, followed by the description of the interior of one of the tombs by way of showing the layout of the others. In the letter, Beulé acknowledges the importance of providing plans and drawings, which were present in his monograph. That the hill containing the tombs was sizeable suggested to Beulé that there would be an abundance of them ('thousands of burial chambers and millions of tombs') concealed in the area, though this would prove to be incorrect.[29] Yet his work, especially ensuring that he published his results quickly and included comparanda (mostly notably tomb typologies from the eastern Mediterranean), showed the way to those who came after him.

In his brief time in Carthage that autumn of 1859, Beulé also took the opportunity to turn to the ports, knowing that he did not have to worry about competition from Davis (see Figure 4.4). In examining this area, Beulé was, as before, looking for Punic remains. Unlike his earlier excavation on the Byrsa hill, however, he needed permission to dig on the site since two ministers of the bey had villas there. The French consul, Roches, was able to gain access for Beulé to the ports with the proviso that everything be put back as it had been. This arrangement had its advantages: the excavations on the Byrsa hill had been plundered in the short time that Beulé had been away (despite the presence of a guard) and such a request, at least, would protect whatever he found from looters. The work at the ports turned out to be extremely difficult due to the waterlogged nature of the site and with fetid mud causing problems,

FIGURE 4.4 *View of the ports, 1884 (Evariste Pricot de Sainte-Marie, 1884).*

but Beulé managed to put in more than 300 small trenches in a two-kilometre circuit. After digging the trenches, he allowed the water to settle, advantageously at the level of the destruction, and thus was able to draw the walls. This enabled him to produce a plan that showed both the circular military port (the Cothon), the island at its centre and the rectangular merchant port south of it (see Plan 1.1 in Chapter 1). Beulé's assessment of the circular harbour has generally stood the test of time, but he believed the rectangular port was much larger than it actually was. This is because the Tophet, which bordered the harbour to the west, had not yet been discovered. After completing his exploration of the ports, Beulé returned to France.

One of the main reasons for the brevity of Beulé's excavations was the lack of financial support. In fact, the subtitle of his 1861 publication makes the situation explicit – that these excavations were undertaken using his own resources. Though he had the backing of Roches and the Academy in Paris, he was unable to attract funding. The Academy had written to the French government on his behalf, arguing that the excavations were in the public interest and requesting 6,000 francs to support the work. They never received a reply. The contrast with the support given by the British government to Davis is notable. In the absence of external funding, Beulé had to cover the costs himself. As Augustus Franks put it at the end of his account of contemporary excavations at Carthage:

> Archaeologists are greatly indebted to M. Beulé for the zeal that led him to make these excavations, which he did solely in the spirit of antiquarian investigation, neither counting the cost nor looking to be rewarded by the discovery of ancient works of art, but simply to obtain a satisfactory

solution of some of the numerous doubts which beset the topography of Carthage.[30]

Shortly after his return to Paris in 1860, the Academy elected Beulé a fellow in recognition of all that he had done in the service of archaeology. This was a great honour, given that he was only thirty-four, and may have gone some way to compensate for the expense he had incurred in his excavations at Carthage. On the other hand, such recognition does not make up for the fact that, in the end, Beulé was unable to do as much as he had wanted. This sense of unfinished business is highlighted by the advice he provides for future excavators (in the conclusion of the section on the Byrsa hill in *Fouilles à Carthage*) on both that site and the ports. He admits that he was only able to produce modest results as a private individual and that government support was crucial for future success. He was critical of contemporaries who were just looking for portable objects – again a dig at Davis, who had himself criticized Beulé for wanting 'to establish his fame upon the authority of a dumb wall'.[31] Beulé emphasized that it was architecture that would provide the most information about the forgotten civilization. His concentration on the built environment added a different dimension to the ancient city. Also hugely helpful was the fact that he published his results, quickly and clearly, which allowed others to build upon his work.

Beulé was astute in his assessment of the challenges of excavating at Carthage in his time, some of which still exist today. He notes the size of the Byrsa hill and the need to differentiate between Punic and Roman remains on the hill, the area of the forum being under cultivation and the region of the ports being in private hands. All of this meant that future excavations would need to be funded by governments, which had the means to provide the required resources since the sum would be substantial. There is a sense of frustration that he was not able to do more, yet what he had managed to accomplish was significant: he had dug deeply enough on the Byrsa hill to reach the burnt remains of houses dating to the final phase of Punic Carthage. This makes Charles-Ernest Beulé the first excavator to have uncovered physical evidence, in situ, of the Punic city on the hill.

5

The French Collector

In November 1862, Gustav Flaubert's novel *Salammbô* was published. An imaginary glimpse into the civilization of Carthage between the First and Second Punic wars, the novel is based mainly on Flaubert's reading of the Greek historian Polybius. It is, perhaps, the ultimate expression of Europe's increasing fascination with the myth and history of Carthage at the time. The choice of topic allowed Flaubert to indulge his long-standing interest in ancient history and he thought it might also provide a refuge from his critics, since few would have any knowledge of the history and culture of Punic Carthage. He could let his imagination run wild, but it is also clear that he was reflecting on his contemporary situation. By focusing on the perceived decadence of an ancient society that had resulted in its downfall, Flaubert was commenting on how he viewed the France of his time.[1] He used Carthage as a mirror to reflect contemporary views on the evolution of cultures and their rise and fall.

Flaubert began to write the novel in September 1857, having consulted close to one hundred works on ancient Carthage, including those of Falbe and Dureau de la Malle.[2] In letters written that year, the author expressed serious anxiety about his work, which culminated in the decision to see the site for himself. He left Paris in April 1858 and reached Tunis two weeks later after a stop in Algeria. Of the six weeks Flaubert would spend in Tunisia, two of those would be in the area around Carthage. When Flaubert first arrived at the site, his guide was none other than Nathan Davis. As Freed notes in her book on Davis, the information – including that Flaubert was a guest at the Davis household – is only provided through Flaubert's own journal entries.[3] Perhaps Davis did not consider him impressive enough or – given the political and national rivalries of the day – considered him too French. Either way the renowned author does not get mentioned alongside other contemporary celebrities in Davis' own work. Flaubert spent four days examining the topography and the archaeological remains at Carthage, though he was more interested in getting a sense of the place, the lay of the land, than in recording in detail what he saw. When he returned to Paris, the author acknowledged that what he had already written would have to be reworked, given what he had learned in North Africa. It seems likely that the sources he had made use of beforehand had not been sufficient for him to imagine a credible depiction of the Punic city.

It took Flaubert another three years to complete *Salammbô*. Upon publication, the book met with mixed reviews. Very few were positive: Flaubert's friend Thèophile Gautier was full of praise for what the author had achieved and Hector Berlioz, the composer of the opera *Les Troyens* (The Trojans), praised Flaubert's archaeological knowledge – as well as his imagination.[4] But a review in *Le Figaro* (December 1862) noted how difficult it was to make sense of the novel, suggesting it was easier for Flaubert to rebuild Carthage than to find readers.[5] One of the most strident critics was a German archaeologist, Wilhelm Fröhner. A curator at the Louvre and known as a collector of antiquities, Fröhner took issue with the historical content of the novel in an article entitled 'Le Roman archéologique en France' (The Archaeological Novel in France).[6] He pointed out that the distinct lack of archaeological evidence about Punic Carthage meant that by presenting the city as he had, Flaubert was being disingenuous. Though he did not often respond to his critics, in this case the author felt he had no choice. In his response to Fröhner (dated 21 January 1863), Flaubert carefully outlined the research that he had done and offered rebuttals to the criticisms. It is from this detailed retort that we can see the extent of Flaubert's research into Carthage and, indeed, what was available at the time to those with an interest in the site.[7] *Salammbô* clearly generated discussion about what was actually known about Punic Carthage in the second half of the nineteenth century. Ever since its publication, the novel has been important in the way that the Punic world has been imagined and exoticized: Salammbô has featured in a wide range of visual media, ranging from paintings and illustrations to video games (see Figure 5.1).

Salammbô also sparked a more general interest in the archaeology of Carthage and its Punic past among the wider public. Indeed, it was Punic

FIGURE 5.1 Salammbô Praying at Carthage *by Jean-Paul Sinibaldi, 1885 (Alamy).*

Carthage that attracted the attention of an interpreter for the Consulate of France in the 1860s and 1870s, Jean-Baptiste-Évariste-Charles Pricot de Sainte-Marie (1843–99). He was the son of Jean-Baptiste-Évariste-Marie Pricot de Sainte-Marie (1810–72), a French officer who specialized in land surveying.[8] The elder Pricot de Sainte-Marie had served the French government in Algeria (1834–8), where land survey and occupation were closely linked in the early years of conquest.[9] While there, he had travelled in Tunisia and, on a trip in 1837, made note of Roman inscriptions. It is possible that he may even have come into contact with Falbe, who was working in Carthage at the time. In 1838, the elder Pricot de Sainte-Marie was sent to Tunisia to work on an official map for the new bey and he would spend much of the next decade there. He was soon on good terms with Ahmed Bey (ruled 1837–55), which provided him with the opportunity to travel widely in the country. His interest in the ancient world meant that his observations added to the knowledge of what was on the ground in Tunisia and his discoveries were presented in 1847 in a work entitled *Antiquités de la Régence de Tunis* (Antiquities of the Regency of Tunis). Though the elder Pricot de Sainte-Marie did not focus exclusively on Carthage in his research, it seems likely that his curiosity was an inspiration for the work of the son.

The younger Pricot de Sainte-Marie worked as an interpreter in Tunis from 1862 to 1864 and then again from 1873 to 1876. During his second appointment, he used his time outside of regular employment to explore the ancient site of Carthage and to undertake archaeological investigations in the city. Pricot de Sainte-Marie was aware of the work that had been carried out in Carthage by those who had been there before, in particular that of Falbe, Davis and Beulé. In fact, in 1875, he published a bibliography of previous research on the site, that was republished, expanded and with corrections, three years later.[10] Of Davis, he, like others, had little good to say, but he considered Falbe and Beulé, along with Dureau de la Malle, as key to understanding the topography of the city. Whereas earlier enthusiasts had been searching for physical evidence of the Punic city, whether architectural or material, Pricot de Sainte-Marie decided to focus specifically on locating Punic and neo-Punic inscriptions. Epigraphy would provide a fruitful avenue into a study of the world of ancient Carthage, but Pricot de Sainte-Marie was also inspired by the new project of the *Corpus Inscriptionum Semiticarum* (Collection of Semitic Inscriptions) started by Ernest Renan in 1867. For the first time, Phoenician, Punic and Neo-Punic inscriptions would be published together as a corpus. Part one of the *CIS* came out in 1881, providing a whole new resource for scholars working in the discipline.

As noted in the discussion on Davis (see Chapter 4), Punic inscriptions were a rarity in the mid-nineteenth century. It is not surprising, then, that Pricot de Sainte-Marie sought to expand knowledge of these important artefacts through collating what was to be found in Carthage and environs. Laporte refers to Pricot de Sainte-Marie's decision to study these inscriptions as bold, since he did not read Punic.[11] As a result, he would find it difficult to assess the importance of what he might find. Nevertheless, Pricot de Sainte-Marie set to work immediately upon his arrival at Carthage in the summer of 1873, sending a copy of a Punic inscription to the Academy in Paris, the body that had oversight for the *CIS*. Impressed with the find, they commissioned him to continue his research, furnishing him with guidelines for what they needed for the publication.

In order to find as many Punic inscriptions as he could, Pricot de Sainte-Marie searched private collections in Tunis and its environs and spoke to anyone interested in antiquities. He was often frustrated because collections had been sold and dispersed, and so were difficult to locate. For example, Françoise Bourgade, the first chaplain of the Chapel of Saint Louis on the Byrsa hill, had published several inscriptions (with translations) in the 1850s.[12] He had also created two collections of antiquities while in Carthage. Pierre Gandolphe, in his history of the site of Saint Louis, considers the collection in the residence provided for Bourgade near the chapel to be the first archaeological museum in the Regency.[13] But upon Bourgade's return to Paris in 1858, these collections were split up: some were sold by the guardian of the chapel to tourists, others were sold at auction to someone described only as a Greek (though the latter inscriptions ended up, for the most part, at the British Museum, as Pricot de Sainte-Marie himself notes). To his credit, Pricot de Sainte-Marie took care to record these inscriptions when it was brought to his attention that they were entering the market or moving into private collections. By March 1874, through sheer persistence, he had managed to examine twelve different collections containing 184 inscriptions and had sent copies of nearly thirty of these to Paris. As a result of his success in finding these inscriptions, he asked for – and was granted – a formal mission by the Academy. His remit was to engage in further research in Carthage, this time through excavation, that would benefit the *CIS*. But the budget was tight and the conditions restrictive: he was only to excavate where inscriptions had been found previously and had to produce a plan of their exact find-spots, along with those found earlier. He was also to send to Paris all stones that were inscribed and to make squeezes and photographs of those that could not be sent. The methodology described for the preservation of the epigraphic information seems sound but there is no doubt that the line between plunder and research continued to be blurred.

Pricot de Sainte-Marie began excavating at Carthage in late August 1874, starting in an area where stelae had been found in the past (see 'A' on his plan, Figure 5.2). He was generally a conscientious excavator, repeatedly expressing concern to the Academy about his methodology. By December 1875, he had excavated in eleven places. Despite clear instructions from Paris about focusing only on stelae, because they were difficult to find, Pricot de Sainte-Marie drifted from this mandate and decided to explore tombs near the La Malga cisterns (see Plan 1.2 in Chapter 1) and also several temples. His techniques were typical of the period, with huge trenches being dug that were left open after excavation. Pricot de Sainte-Marie kept a daily journal that formed the basis of his 1884 publication, *Mission à Carthage* (Mission to

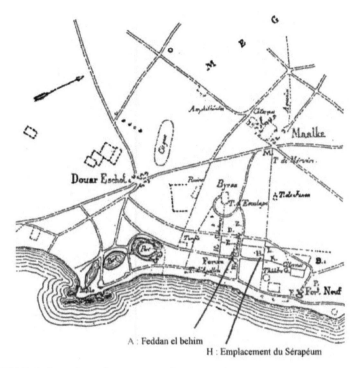

A : Feddan el behim

H : Emplacement du Sérapéum

FIGURE 5.2 *Location of excavations by Pricot de Sainte-Marie (Evariste Pricot de Sainte-Marie, 1884).*

Carthage).[14] He was careful to plot the location of every inscription he found, which suggests a meticulousness that had been lacking in some of his predecessors. The final report provided an enormous amount of detail, though it was somewhat overwhelming, and the result is a systematic record of the state of the ruins in Carthage at the time Pricot de Sainte-Marie was working.

Two of the sites excavated proved especially fruitful. At location 'H' on his plan, Pricot de Sainte-Marie discovered the Serapeum. This was a temple to the god Serapis, a hybrid Romano-Egyptian deity that had gained widespread importance and popularity during the Roman Empire.[15] The identification of the site as a temple to Serapis was later confirmed by epigraphic evidence. At the Serapeum, Pricot de Sainte-Marie uncovered a marble head of the second-century Roman emperor Hadrian and a still extant statue of his wife, the empress Sabina. The head of Hadrian was later sent to the National Museum of Antiquities in Algiers, while the statue of Sabina would make its way to the Louvre. The exact location of the temple remains rather vague because subsequent construction of the commuter rail line destroyed the visible ruins. But it seems to have been situated between the Byrsa and Juno hills, near the intersection of the modern Rue Kennedy and Rue Tanit, just to the north of the modern line of the TGM (see Plan 5.1).[16]

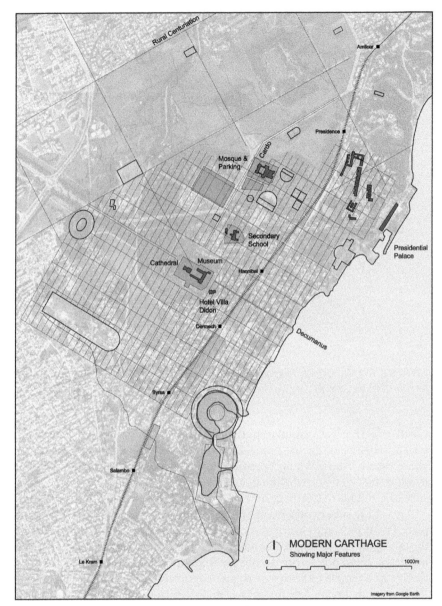

PLAN 5.1 *Modern Carthage (drawn by Stephen Copp).*

Even more relevant for his interest in epigraphy, Pricot de Sainte-Marie
found over 2,000 Punic stelae, most of them inscribed, at location 'A' (see
Figure 5.2). In order to gain access to this area, he removed several walls,
but was careful to record whatever he demolished. Such was the quantity of
epigraphic finds from this location that Pricot de Sainte-Marie began to

worry he might not discover any more Punic inscriptions in Carthage or, at least, would not be able to process them. He thought it safer to turn his attention to Utica (see Map 1.2 in Chapter 1), where he worked for two months (from December 1875 to January 1876). In 1876, he was provided with additional funds by the French government to return to Carthage, but before he could get back to do more excavation, he was promoted to vice-consul and transferred to Dalmatia.

The total number of Punic inscriptions from Carthage discovered by Pricot de Sainte-Marie was approximately 2,200, a substantial – and unexpected – number. He had made copies of all of these, but his instructions were to send to Paris all those that were inscribed and that could be shipped. This accounted for such a sizeable proportion of the finds that he ran into some operational problems. No one had expected so many inscriptions to be found and no one was certain what to do with them all. In fact, as early as September 1874, shortly after he had started excavating, Pricot de Sainte-Marie was asked by the Louvre to stop sending finds. His final shipment arrived at the museum that November, and a month later, the Louvre reported that they had no room for any more stelae. Their reluctance seems to have stemmed partly from the sheer volume but also the fact that these were Punic inscriptions. The French government was also beginning to balk at the transportation costs. But, in a turn that seems quite modern, once the story was picked up by the press, the museum became more accommodating. There was, it seems, room for the inscriptions but no money for their shipment. As the situation dragged on, Pricot de Sainte-Marie grew increasingly anxious in case the Tunisian government should place an embargo on the export of all finds. The growing autonomy of elite Tunisians and their engagement with the wider Mediterranean world meant that at this time there was an increasing interest in their own national heritage. For example, shortly after Davis and Beulé had finished excavating at Carthage, Sidi Mohamed Khaznadar, the son of Mustapha Khaznadar, the first minister of the bey, had been given what Pricot de Sainte-Marie refers to as a 'monopoly' over antiquities in the country. What this meant in practical terms was that Khaznadar started depositing finds in the garden of his father's residence at Manouba (a neighbourhood of Tunis) in what amounted to a private museum. Foreigners who were excavating in the country were now required to surrender part of what they found to his collection. Yet Khaznadar was not averse to selling finds to those who visited the country, whether for their own collections or for museums. Legislation had been put in place to stop the shipment of antiquities from Algeria to Paris as early as 1850. In Tunisia a similar embargo would not be introduced until 1886.

Pricot de Sainte-Marie had to wait for nearly a year before the transportation of his finds was organized. This came about only after intercession by the Academy with the proper government authorities in Paris. Preparations were made to send 2,083 stelae along with the statue of Sabina and a few other pieces. Transport was arranged on the ship the

Magenta, which set out at the end of September 1875. A month later, on 30 October, the ship dropped anchor at Toulon but arrived too late in the evening to begin unloading. During the night, a fire started which burned extremely hot for three hours before the ship finally exploded. It seemed that most of the finds would be lost. For the next two months, divers worked to recover what they could from the cargo. In January 1876, four boxes were sent to Paris which contained 1,571 stelae and the statue of Sabina, minus the head. A description of the finds notes that the condition of the stones varied from dark staining to extensive friability. A complete inventory of what had been recovered was undertaken by Philippe Berger in 1876 and the story of the stelae was told in the first volume of the *CIS*. Thankfully, Pricot de Sainte-Marie, as requested, had made copies of all the stones he found – without his diligence much of the information about this collection would have been lost. More of the cargo, including the head of the Sabina statue, was brought to the surface in the 1990s in a salvage expedition led by Max Guérout of the Naval Archaeology Research Group at the request of the French Ministry of Culture.[17] The Louvre now displays the charred head of Sabina in a case beside the statue.

Pricot de Sainte-Marie published extensively over the course of his time in Tunisia. One of his most accessible works is a 'handbook' to the ruins of Carthage, published in the weekly paper *L'Explorateur* (The Explorer) in January of 1876. The aim was to guide visitors through the site, starting at the Chapel of Saint Louis and leading them through the Punic, Roman and Christian ruins that could be discerned. At eighteen pages including illustrations and maps, one gets an idea of how little there was to see and also of what the contemporary thinking was about Punic Carthage. Despite all that had been learned, the handbook still included the Punic period Temple of Asclepius and the possible palace of Dido on the Byrsa hill that are only referred to in the ancient literary sources. There is no material evidence for these structures even today. The major publication of Pricot de Sainte-Marie's work at the site, *Mission à Carthage*, was published in 1884. In eleven chapters, he gives a comprehensive look at how he went about his excavations and provides information about all his finds, and in particular, the inscriptions. He furnishes details on where the material ended up and finally looks at the topography of Carthage and provides plans of the city. Among those who had come before him, he mentions the usual personalities: Shaw, Humbert, Falbe and Dureau de la Malle. The book is lavishly illustrated, including both drawings and engravings of finds (see Figure 5.3). There are also photographs of various vistas in Carthage (see Figure 4.4 in Chapter 4). Some near contemporary reviews of the book were not all that positive. In his work on Carthage, Audollent criticized Pricot de Sainte-Marie for including his correspondence with the Academy and for the huge amount of detail and the trivial amount of interpretation in the chapter on topography.[18] Others complained about the delay in publication and the techniques employed in the field. The delay was not the fault of the author:

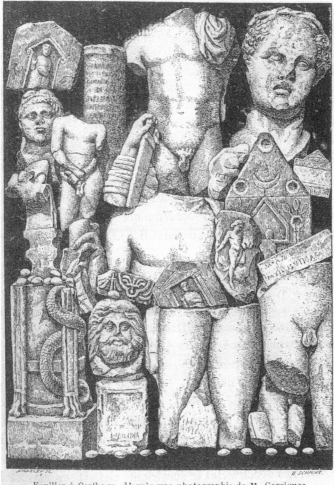

Fouilles à Carthage, d'après une photographie de M. Garrigues.

FIGURE 5.3 *Engraving of a selection of finds from Pricot de Sainte-Marie's excavations (Evariste Pricot de Sainte-Marie, 1884).*

Pricot de Saint-Marie had finished the book in 1878 but the government turned out to be reluctant to pay for its publication. As for his methodology, given the period, it is not surprising to have successors scrutinize the activities of those who had worked in the field before them and to be critical.

For Pricot de Sainte-Marie himself, what he had accomplished in Carthage was of great importance. That significance was commemorated by his family in a marble plaque in the Chapel of Saint Louis at Carthage on the Byrsa hill, which read, 'To the memory of M. Pricot de Sainte-Marie former consul general and in remembrance of his work in Tunisia and his discoveries at Carthage (1874–1876). His family 1899.' Pricot de Sainte-Marie had been instrumental in providing Punic inscriptions for inclusion in the *CIS* and he was diligent in sending copies to Paris. Indeed, his meticulous recording of the inscriptions meant that the disaster of the *Magenta* was not more deeply felt. Pricot de Sainte-Marie was careful to produce maps showing where he had excavated and he also made plans of any structure that he was dismantling to get to the inscriptions. Although we can lament the level of destruction, it also reveals how the quest for Punic material could outweigh all other considerations in the field.

The mid-1870s marked the beginning of a new era of excavation at Carthage, with the arrival of Les Pères Blancs (White Fathers). The Catholic Church had a strong interest in the site, given its connection with many great Christians of antiquity, in particular Tertullian, St Cyprian and St Augustine. In 1875, Cardinal Charles Lavigerie, Archbishop of Algiers, was granted the guardianship of the Chapel of Saint Louis in Carthage on behalf of the White Fathers, a group he had founded in 1868 partly to promote Christianity in North Africa.[19] Lavigerie viewed the role of custodian of the chapel as an opportunity to expand the influence of the Catholic Church in Tunisia. This is best exemplified in a physical sense by the construction of the Cathedral of Saint Louis, alongside the chapel, in the 1880s (see Figure 5.4). The first stone laid for the cathedral came from the basilica of Damous-el-Karita, in a symbolic association with Carthage's Christian past. Consecrated on 15 May 1890 and with Lavigerie having been named the Archbishop of Carthage and Algiers, Primate of Africa, the cathedral was from that time the main church in North Africa. In addition to promoting the Catholic Church, Lavigerie had in mind that the White Fathers would be able to advance French interests in Carthage. This brotherhood of Catholic priests thus became active in Tunisia at a pivotal moment in the country's history.

For almost a century, the ruling beys of Tunis had kept the Ottomans at a distance, to the best of their ability. Their relationship with foreign powers had largely been cordial and with the French in particular it was one of mutual advantage and support. Starting in the 1860s, however, a series of events shifted the precarious balance of power. Unrest in Tunisia in 1864 and then serious financial problems in the later part of that decade created a political crisis. In addition, the French territorial losses in the Franco-Prussian War of 1870 made France more eager to safeguard their interests in North Africa, especially in Algeria. At the same time, French citizens' financial investments (especially in agriculture) in Tunisia meant that those whose interests were at risk demanded protection for their investments. Finally, there was the sharp decline in Ottoman influence as a result of their defeat at the hands of the Russians in the Russo-Turkish War of 1877–8. All of these developments led the French to re-evaluate their position in Tunisia. The Congress of Berlin of 1878 saw the major European powers (Austria-Hungary, Prussia [Germany], Britain, France and Italy) vying for influence over the ever-diminishing holdings of the Ottoman Empire in the Mediterranean. At this crucial meeting, the French were able to negotiate

FIGURE 5.4 *Cathedral and monastery on the Byrsa hill (postcard, authors' collection).*

international support for France having a greater role in Tunisia. They did not want to have outright sovereignty over the country because of the expense and the optics and the status of a protectorate was deemed less colonial, though of course it was nothing of the sort. A protectorate still imposed foreign rule on a country and at that country's expense. Lord Salisbury, the British Foreign Secretary who attended the Congress with Prime Minister Benjamin Disraeli, made a telling comment to his counterpart, the French foreign minister, Monsieur Waddington, in a private conversation. Salisbury was reported to have said, 'Take Tunis if you like . . . in any case, you could not leave Carthage in the hands of the barbarians.'[20] This sums up the prevailing attitude held by the colonial powers in Europe towards North Africa, but also illustrates the way that Carthage still featured in contemporary conceptualization of the space at the very highest levels of government.

Three years later, in the spring of 1881, and using the excuse of disturbances in the country, the French invaded Tunisia and forced Mohammed al-Sadiq Bey to submit to their control. He was coerced into signing the Treaty of Bardo, which handed over 'security' in Tunisia to the French government in what was the beginning of the occupation.[21] The protectorate was officially installed in June 1883 by the Convention of La Marsa, which allowed France to become involved in all internal matters, completely sidelining Ali Bey, who had taken over as ruler after the death of his brother the previous October. The position of French Resident-General was first established to oversee security and foreign matters. A key player in this role was Paul Cambon, who was appointed early in 1882 and was instrumental both in the creation of the protectorate and in the direction it took until his departure in 1886. Pressure on France to establish a protectorate had also come from the Catholic Church, which pushed for greater access to Tunisia. In 1881, shortly after the signing of the Treaty of Bardo, Lavigerie was appointed the Apostolic Administrator of the Vicariate of Tunis and he worked closely with French government officials (including Cambon) over the next two years in the establishment of the protectorate. Lavigerie was a great advocate for France extending its power overseas, but it was also the case that the White Fathers would be able to avoid French anticlerical laws under a protectorate in Tunisia. The separation of Church and State had been a contentious issue for a least a century and Lavigerie no doubt was concerned about the effect any move to enact such a policy might have on his mission if it applied to Tunisia. In fact, it took until December 1905 before such a law was enacted in France, but it did not apply to the protectorate. The White Fathers had by then proven themselves too important in their role of advancing France's interests in Tunisia to be affected.

This, then, marked the beginning of a long association between the White Fathers and Carthage. One of the ways in which Lavigerie sought to consolidate the Church's hold on the area was through archaeology, in particular, concerning that of the early Church. Lavigerie had been a professor of the history of Christianity at the Sorbonne, so his interest was not surprising. But he also saw archaeology as an opportunity to restore the Church in the region through an association with the ancient Christian city. When he sent missionaries to Carthage in 1875, Lavigerie told them that they should concentrate their studies on two things: Arabic and the archaeology of the city. And he became a meticulous overseer of the excavations undertaken by the White Fathers, including the publications produced. Moreover, just before the creation of the protectorate in 1883, Lavigerie had sent a communiqué to the Academy in Paris in which he argued for a permanent archaeological mission at Carthage. In this communiqué, he showcased some of the recent work done at the site, highlighting in particular the study of the topography of the site, the discovery of the cemetery of the slaves of the Roman imperial household and the unearthing of an early Christian cemetery.[22] The following year, the creation of a department of antiquities was mooted but it was not until 1885 that such a body was established by the French and Tunisian governments to regulate excavation in Tunisia. Thus, through his promotion of archaeology at Carthage, Lavigerie opened up the site to wide-ranging exploration and he remained actively involved in this endeavour until his death in November 1892. He was buried in the cathedral on the Byrsa hill and remained there until its deconsecration in 1964, when his body was taken to Rome.

6

The Excavating Priest

More than any other individual, Father Alfred-Louis Delattre (1850–1932) is associated with Lavigerie's mission in Tunisia and its archaeological agenda (see Figure 6.1). Ordained in 1874, Delattre arrived in Carthage a year later. He would be active at the site for over fifty years and his influence can be seen on most of the excavations of this period. His long tenure also meant that he was part of the transition from the early archaeological explorations characterized by Davis and Beulé to the more modern processes seen, for example, with the American Francis Kelsey at the Tophet (see Chapter 7). Delattre's own excavations are a mix of the two: he made many notes and published prolifically, although the analysis was often rushed and superficial. Throughout his time in the area, Delattre remained an enthusiastic advocate for the archaeology of the ancient city. His interest would be expanded far beyond the Christian remains that Lavigerie had promoted, to touch almost all of ancient Carthage's phases of occupation.[1]

Key to Delattre's success in the field was the relationship he cultivated with the local population. His charity work focused on the needs of the locals who, when they learned of his interest in all things archaeological, would bring him objects (a fragment of inscription or small finds) that they normally would have sold to tourists. As a result, Delattre was able to understand the topography of the site better and indeed to figure out where he might most successfully excavate. As any archaeologist knows, local knowledge is key to success. He also made use of the work of those who had excavated before him at Carthage. Underlying his success was the status of Tunisia as a protectorate of France after 1883 and the influence of the Church in the area, which guaranteed complete access to any site he wished to explore. Furthermore, the White Fathers often purchased land of interest to them, something that earlier excavators had not been able to do. As encouraged by Lavigerie (and through his own interests as a priest), Delattre primarily focused his attention on the Christian monuments of Carthage. One of the most important buildings for the Christian faith was a Roman civic building, the amphitheatre (see Plan 1.2 in Chapter 1).[2] It was thought to have been the site of the martyrdom of Saints Perpetua and Felicity, two of the most famous Christian martyrs of North Africa, in 203 CE.[3] Once one of the largest amphitheatres in the Roman world (seating *c.* 30,000 people), much of the

FIGURE 6.1 *Delattre at the Chapel of Saint Louis (postcard; courtesy J. J. Rossiter).*

monument had been robbed for construction elsewhere. It may have still been standing to a considerable height at the time of el Idrisi's writing on Carthage in the twelfth century, and other Arabic sources mention its decoration as well. By the middle of the nineteenth century, however, visitors to Carthage noted that there was almost nothing left to see of the structure.

The land was purchased by the White Fathers and, over several years beginning in 1895, Delattre undertook the excavation of the site. He had a specific reason for focusing on the amphitheatre at this time, connected to the 1700th anniversary of the famous martyrdoms. Delattre wanted to make the site a showcase for ecclesiastical visitors. It is not known for certain what modifications were made to the site at this time, but the arena was cleared and a portion of the arena wall reconstructed, along with parts of the two walls outside that wall. Delattre also built a chapel to the martyrs in the centre of the amphitheatre, with concrete steps to allow public access to the subterranean area (see Figure 6.2). There were regular reports on the excavation in both academic and non-academic journals. For example, in 1897, Antoine Héron de Villefosse, curator at the Louvre and an enthusiastic supporter of Delattre, reported to the Academy that the excavations had cleared one of the many corridors of the arena and had also determined the width of the amphitheatre.[4] In 1898, Delattre noted in a report submitted to the *American Journal of Archaeology* that he had revealed the entire arena and had discovered the foundations of most of the building as well as several architectural fragments. Among the finds were fifty-five fascinating lead curse tablets that were later published by Auguste Audollent.[5] But nowhere did Delattre include details of the reconstruction he undertook, not even in his longer publications on the amphitheatre. In his eagerness to clear the arena and have everything ready for the anniversary of the martyrdoms, evidence for the later periods was destroyed, much as we have seen with those excavating in Carthage earlier in the century.

FIGURE 6.2 *Amphitheatre at Carthage (photo by Eve MacDonald).*

From the outset, the buildings of Christian Carthage were a primary focus for the White Fathers. Foremost among these were a group of early Christian basilicas located outside of the city walls: Damous-el-Karita, the Basilica Maiorum at Mcidfa and the basilicas of Bir el Knissia and Bir Ftouha (see Plan 1.2 in Chapter 1). Delattre started his exploration of Christian Carthage at Damous-el-Karita, the largest of these basilicas, located near the Odeon hill, excavation beginning in 1881. He initially explored the early Christian cemetery, followed by the basilica and adjoining buildings. A lack of funds meant that progress was slow, but Delattre continued working on the site for a decade. Regular updates on the excavations were sent to correspondents and these were reported in journals such as the French *Comptes rendus des séances de l'Académie des Inscriptions et Belles-Lettres* (Reports of the Sessions of the Academy of Inscriptions and Belles-Lettres) and the *American Journal of Archaeology*.[6] In 1891, Delattre himself presented a paper on the basilica at a conference in Paris. Such publicity was no doubt partly an attempt at securing funding for future excavation and Delattre continued to publish material from the site for many years, including more than 3,500 inscriptions found in the cemetery. In 1920, the columns that had been found at Damous-el-Karita were re-erected and five years later, reconstruction of the walls was carried out. This took place thanks to the support of an unnamed wealthy American. Such an endeavour enabled Delattre to produce a plan of the basilica. In addition, eight years earlier and to the southwest of the basilica, he had discovered a subterranean rotunda and a large rectangular building associated with the structure. A 1912 publication by Delattre provided plans of these buildings as well as photographs of the excavation and a full description of the burials discovered. Though he described the rotunda as an 'archaeological curiosity', Delattre suggested it might be a baptistery. These buildings have recently been re-examined and are now identified as a martyrium of Byzantine date.[7]

In the early twentieth century, Delattre continued to focus almost exclusively on Christian Carthage. The Basilica Maiorum was excavated between 1906 and 1908, Delattre again first turning his attention to the cemetery associated with the structure after which he explored the surrounding area. He uncovered evidence for a grand basilica, though most of it had been destroyed. Of great interest were several funerary inscriptions with the name 'Vibius'. Given that the martyred Saint Perpetua's full name was Vibia Perpetua, this led Delattre to conclude that he had found her martyrium, though recently this association has been challenged. In the 1920s, Delattre was involved in more projects associated with the Christian city, publishing inscriptions from a large basilica near Sainte-Monique that he thought was associated with St Cyprian. The definitive publication of these inscriptions was produced by Liliane Ennabli in a series of monographs from 1975 to 1991. In addition, Delattre worked on the sites of the basilicas of Bir el Knissia and Bir Ftouha. He first identified the former of these as a

Christian site in the late nineteenth century because of the number of Christian inscriptions in the area. Finally examined in 1922–3, the building had been robbed out, but there was enough on the ground for a plan to be made, which was reproduced at the time on a postcard for sale in the museum. Although he never published his investigations of Bir el Knissia, Delattre's field notes survived, allowing an American team under the direction of Susan T. Stevens to re-excavate the site in the early 1990s making use of the earlier evidence.[8] The second of these basilicas, Bir Ftouha, had come to Delattre's attention in 1880 when he recognized what he thought was a baptistery.[9] Part of the site was excavated in the late 1890s by Paul Gauckler, at that time director of the Department of Antiquities, who removed several Christian mosaics. It was only in the early 1920s that Delattre himself began to dig there. He excavated the west end of the site but not the basilica itself and brought to light several Roman sarcophagi in the five years that he worked there. Although Delattre believed that the basilica at Bir Ftouha had been built as a memorial to St Cyprian, there is nothing tangible to connect the two. The desire to associate remains with the ancient Christian martyrs (or texts) echoes what we have seen with those who searched for Punic remains as well. That such influential early Christians as Tertullian, St Cyprian or St Augustine were associated closely with Carthage meant that the White Fathers were enthusiastic in their attempts to make connections to these individuals, with or without the evidence.

It is important to remember that, even given the rudimentary methodology of the time, Delattre's excavations meant that these sites were not lost in the coming decades. A rail line linking Tunis with La Marsa began running in 1872. Updated with a tram line in 1907 – known as the Tunis–Goulette–Marsa or TGM – it cut right through much of the ancient city (see Plan 5.1 in Chapter 5). Such improved transportation links with Tunis accelerated construction of prosperous neighbourhoods in and around Carthage. Other projects in the second half of the nineteenth century, such as the laying of pipes to bring water to the city from the spring at Zaghouan (about 70 kilometres away), also meant that archaeological sites were put at risk. This was noted by William N. Bates in a comment made in 1912: 'At Carthage, modern enterprise has obliterated the Phoenician city and threatens the Roman part with a similar fate.'[10] The early archaeologists may have been reckless, with a lack of attention to detail compared to current methodologies, but much that is known about ancient Carthage today is a testament to what they did manage to uncover. During those boom years in the late nineteenth and early twentieth centuries, their work meant that what might have disappeared was at least recorded and noted down.

It was not only Christian Carthage that the White Fathers concentrated on – they also pursued an active interest in the Punic city. In 1878, with the specific encouragement of Lavigerie, Delattre undertook test excavations on the Hill of Juno that revealed Punic tombs. In the coming years, he excavated several Punic cemeteries, including those on the Byrsa (1880–3), at Douïmès

(1892–6, and again briefly in 1907) and at an area referred to as 'near Sainte-Monique', which was close to Bordj Djedid (1898–1905) (see Plan 1.1 in Chapter 1). This was the first attempt at a systematic investigation of the Punic cemeteries at Carthage.[11] The tombs provided a glimpse into the world of Punic Carthage available nowhere else and are still of great significance to our understanding of the culture. In 1905, Mabel Moore published a report on these sites in English and noted in her preface that:

> [m]odern excavation in the Punic Tombs of Carthage has given this people an opportunity of at last speaking for themselves, and it is to this voice from the grave that we now have to hearken, straining our ears with patient sympathy, as the pick-axes of the monks of Carthage proceed to liberate the stifled spirit of the past.[12]

The depth at which these tombs were found – some as deep as 14 metres – made excavation extremely difficult. Before long, Delattre began using a horizontal trench for ease of access, as reported in the *Revue Archéologique* in January/February 1891. From the site near Sainte-Monique, Delattre excavated four unique marble anthropoid sarcophagi, two of which are now in the Louvre, the others in the Carthage Museum (see Figure 6.3). Delattre himself tells the story of the discovery of one of these sarcophagi and the dramatic methodology used to extract them. While he was celebrating the feast of the Counter-Reformation Saint Charles Borromée (4 November 1902), he was summoned immediately to the cemetery. Delattre did not hesitate to leave the celebration and go directly to the site where he was then lowered down into a shaft in his full priestly garb. The depth of the shaft was 13 metres and with the use of a pulley managed by the workmen (see Figure 6.4), he came upon a marble sarcophagus of outstanding quality which had been covered by two wooden coffins. Significantly, Delattre's examination of these sites demonstrated that the cemeteries corresponded to the limits of the ancient Punic city, which in turn encouraged further exploration of the Punic city – for example at Dermech, by Paul Gauckler (1899–1902).

One of the most productive sites Delattre excavated was the Cemeteries of the Officials, located near the amphitheatre (see Plan 1.2 in Chapter 1). Excavated on three separate occasions between 1880 and 1898, they produced nearly 1,000 inscriptions of slaves and freedmen of the imperial household associated with the procurator in Carthage and dating from the first to the third centuries CE.[13] Delattre seemed uninterested in the tombs themselves, though he published the inscriptions in various journals and magazines. Furthermore, on the Byrsa and near the Antonine Baths (see Plan 1.2 in Chapter 1), he excavated the so-called 'amphora walls', which were constructed of Roman period debris – as the name suggests, mostly amphorae fragments. But Delattre was more interested in the information to be gleaned from the writing on these fragments than analysis of the amphorae themselves.[14]

CARTHAGE — Epoque Punique · Les deux Sarcophages du Prêtre
et de la Prêtresse, dans la Chambre Funéraire

FIGURE 6.3 *Punic sarcophagi in situ (postcard; authors' collection).*

Given the importance of Carthage in the history of Christianity, the focus on Christian sites by Delattre and the White Fathers is understandable. There was also an intensive effort to convert the local population and it may have been thought that impressive material remains would enhance this project. With Punic remains, there was also a novelty factor involved. They were only to be found at Carthage, while Roman remains could be found elsewhere and there were others excavating at the same time who were focused on the Roman city – at the Antonine Baths, for example, as well as at the Roman theatre and the odeon (a space used for musical performances; see Plan 1.2 in Chapter 1). So Delattre's lack of interest in the Roman city is not surprising. Nevertheless, he was an enthusiastic excavator and tended to publish his results quickly. Details of his excavations along with descriptions of finds were conveyed in letters regularly sent to members of the Academy in Paris.[15] Freed has noted that this provided Delattre with a measure of influence, important since Delattre lacked academic authority himself.[16]

FIGURE 6.4 *Excavating a Punic sarcophagus (postcard; authors' collection).*

Summaries of this correspondence were then published in various journals such as the *Revue Archéologique* or the *American Journal of Archaeology*. Delattre himself published in both scholarly journals and popular magazines such as *Cosmos* and *Missions Catholiques*. As catalogued by Freed, these articles total well in excess of 500. Though they were often just short notes, by publishing in media that reached such a varied audience, Delattre was able to generate widespread interest in ancient Carthage. He also sold offprints of his articles in the shop of the Carthage Museum, alongside guidebooks to the site for those who visited, in order to raise funds for future work (in 1945, these publications were still available from the 'souvenir counter in the Roman Hall').

In considering all of Delattre's activities in Carthage, perhaps the most long-lasting is his creation of a museum located in the headquarters of the White Fathers on the Byrsa hill.[17] Established in 1875 shortly after Delattre started excavating, it was initially called the Museum of Saint Louis but was renamed in honour of Lavigerie in 1899 (the museum would become the

Carthage National Museum in 1956). The museum had rooms dedicated to the Punic city, the Christian city (i.e., the Roman city) and the Crusades (!), with various pieces of sculpture displayed in the gardens. In a letter to the Academy in 1881, Lavigerie praised Delattre for all that he had accomplished without much support, noting that, after only five years, there were some 6,347 artefacts in the museum.[18] By 1900, the museum contained well over a million items as shown in an illustrated catalogue (in three volumes) produced by Delattre that year. The types of artefacts housed in the museum can be gauged from the report of a robbery that took place in 1889. A list was published in the *American Journal of Archaeology* in March of that year to help with identification of objects that might already be held by or be offered to European museums and collections. The missing artefacts included coins, seals and engraved stones, as well as rings, plaques and various objects in a range of materials – gold, silver, glass, ivory and marble. Such a wide array attests to the richness of the site and to the dedication of Delattre in assembling the collection. It also serves as a reminder that Carthaginian artefacts were of considerable value at the time. It is of note that, a year after the museum on the Byrsa hill had been established (1876), the concept of an archaeological museum in Tunis open to the public and showcasing materials from the entire country was proposed by the new first minister, Kheireddine Pacha. The collection of Sidi Mohamed Khaznadar (as noted in Chapter 5) had been a private endeavor, which meant that few had access. In 1876, the plan was to include Khaznadar's collection, which had been confiscated by the state in 1874, in the museum, as well as materials from excavations in the rest of Tunisia. Unfortunately, Kheireddine Pacha resigned in 1877 before the museum could be realized but he had laid the groundwork for the future. After he stepped down, materials intended for the museum were put into storage in Tunis. These later seem to have been dispersed, with objects ending up in various museums including the British Museum and the Louvre. It would take another decade before a museum of the sort envisioned by Pacha was in operation, with the Alaoui (later Bardo) Museum opening in Tunis in 1888, where a number of artefacts from the original collection were on display.

In the late nineteenth century, tensions had begun to surface between Church and State about the oversight of archaeology in Carthage. The decree that established the Alaoui Museum in 1882 also announced measures to protect antiquities, but it took until 1885 for a such a body to be created. The Service des Antiquités, Beaux-Arts et Monuments historiques en Tunisie (Department of Antiquities, Fine Arts and Historical Monuments in Tunisia) was ostensibly a joint venture between the Tunisian and French authorities with the remit to protect the historic monuments of Tunisia, though the protectorate clearly had greater authority given the political situation at the time. The first director was René du Coudray de La Blanchère, who had worked in Algeria prior to coming to Tunisia. He would hold the post for five years (1885–90). The establishment of such a unit meant that there would now be greater control over archaeological activities throughout the country. With respect to Carthage, there was particular concern about the monopoly that the White Fathers – and Delattre especially – had had on excavation in the area since their establishment there by Lavigerie. How much of this unease on the part of the State was due to anticlerical views at the time is not entirely clear, but there was a definite reluctance to let things continue as they had been. Therefore, the new body would now manage excavations in Carthage, which was bound to cause some friction between the authorities and those excavating. Furthermore, in 1886 a decree was passed which restricted the ownership of antiquities and ensured their preservation. In line with this regulation, La Blanchère had the idea of trying to prise the Museum of Saint Louis away from the White Fathers and bring it under the auspices of the Department of Antiquities. While he was unsuccessful in his attempt, it showed the direction in which things were heading. The act of 1886 also banned the export of antiquities unless written permission was given. That this prohibition may not have had much effect is shown by the presence of artefacts from Carthage in the Gołuchów Castle Museum, part of the Polish National Museum in Poznań. Recent research has shown that these were given by Delattre to Princess Izabela Działyńska, who was a well-known collector of antiquities and whose collection formed the basis for the Gołuchów Castle Museum.[19] Letters from Delattre dated to May 1895 indicate that he had sent the antiquities as a gift because of donations the Princess had made to the White Fathers' work in Carthage. It is clear from the correspondence that much of what was sent came from Delattre's own excavations that year, perhaps from Douïmès. Even with the restrictions in place, it is clear that export of antiquities continued, even to private individuals.

Given the new restrictions, it is not surprising that the relationship between Delattre and the directors of the Department of Antiquities was quite fraught, as evidenced in particular in the letters of La Blanchère's successor, Paul Gauckler. Gauckler had been associated with the Department of Antiquities since 1892 and took over as director in 1896. His excavations in Carthage included Punic, Roman and Christian elements of the city, with articles detailing his work on Punic cemeteries collected and published posthumously as *Nécropoles puniques à Carthage* (1915). He excavated two of the most significant Roman buildings in Carthage: the odeon in 1900 and the theatre in 1904–5 (see Plan 1.2 in Chapter 1).[20] Dating to the second century CE, the theatre seated nearly 12,000 spectators. Gauckler revealed a substantial portion of the structure, including the stage and much of the seating. Reconstruction began almost immediately, with the objective of once more holding dramatic productions on the site. The impetus came from the use of Roman theatres for performances in France, for example at Orange, such events proving to be very popular. It was not Gauckler who was behind this project, though, but an individual named Louis Carton. A medical doctor attached to the French military, Carton had been in Carthage since 1886 and had a keen interest in archaeology. He worked at various sites in Tunisia until his death in 1924 and published extensively, but he saw himself in competition with both Delattre and especially with Gauckler, which meant there was much tension. Carton preferred to see archaeology as a way to emphasize the connection of the French colonialists to the ancient city, but he was also interested in using the site to attract tourists as a way of bolstering the economy. Perhaps more significantly, he recognized the importance of preserving Carthage from development, which was far-sighted for his time. Carton used many different initiatives to achieve his objectives, not only excavation but also a wider engagement with the public. Performances at the theatre were part of this overall strategy.

The first *fêtes de Carthage* took place in 1906 and 1907, under the auspices of the Institut de Carthage.[21] This body had been created in 1893 with the objective of promoting Tunisia, and Carton was its current president. A full account of the opening spectacle was provided in the journal *Revue Tunisienne*, the publication of the Institute, in 1906. The article makes clear the sumptuousness of the performances, showcasing the large number of people taking part as well as the elaborate costuming and set design. It is clear from the discussion that these productions were not only intended to draw in the tourists and to draw attention to the importance of the site of Carthage. They also served to remind the audience of France's inheritance of the Roman city and to promote the influence of French culture in Tunisia. Such was the success of these spectacles that the theatre would be used for other productions throughout the period of the protectorate. Perhaps the most famous cameo, though, was by Winston Churchill, who addressed British troops in the theatre during the Second World War (see Figure 6.5). In an independent Tunisia, various types of performances including music and theatre alongside film viewings continued to take place in the theatre. As a result, in order to accommodate the requirements for modern staging of such events, the structure was heavily restored in the second half of the twentieth century and little of the original Roman theatre is now apparent to the casual observer.

During his tenure as Director of Antiquities, Gauckler oversaw a number of advances, in particular the transition to more scientific excavation in the field. Like La Blanchère, Gauckler also had concerns about the role of the Church in the archaeology of Carthage. In asserting his authority, he had a somewhat uneasy relationship with Delattre.[22] Though Gauckler probably had great admiration for the work of Delattre, he also was eager to reduce the power that the Church had with respect to the ancient site and he was resentful of the influence that the White Fathers had with those managing the protectorate. For his part, Delattre was distrustful of Gauckler. He had had complete freedom in Carthage up to the time of the establishment of the Department of Antiquities and oversight of his work was unwelcome.

Delattre had many supporters, far and wide, who rallied to his assistance when needed. For example, René Cagnat, an influential archaeologist in Paris, wrote to express support for Delattre in 1898 after several battles with the director. Cagnat's words are worth considering:

Our rule has always been to leave you master of the terrain of Carthage, because it was yours before any of us set foot in Tunisia, because you have conquered it by your labour, and because we think the land is large enough that it is not useful to get in one another's way.[23]

The division of spoils and expression of ownership and occupation – and disregard for Tunisian sovereignty – is striking. The letter is an endorsement of Delattre's position and an acknowledgement that some accommodation should be made given the current state of affairs with Gauckler, with the competitive and proprietary nature of archaeological investigation at Carthage clearly emphasized.

Delattre was worried that Gauckler would try to take over the museum in Carthage too, as La Blanchère had earlier planned, and his fear was not without cause. In a letter to his superiors in 1903, Gauckler argued that the government should place the museum under State control. Yet again, however, the will to do this was lacking, since Gauckler was not supported by anyone in power in his attempt. This speaks to the authority that the Church continued to have in Carthage, despite the key role now played by the Department of Antiquities. In fact, the museum would remain in the hands of

FIGURE 6.5 *British Prime Minister Winston Churchill in the theatre at Carthage (1943) (© Imperial War Museums).*

the Church until 1964, several years after Tunisia had become independent in 1956. In the letters to his superiors, Gauckler often expressed his frustration at having to deal with the White Fathers. In particular, he was troubled by the Church's ownership of land in Carthage. As the area continued to be developed because of its prime location so close to Tunis, property prices had increased and there was a fear that this might result in sites being lost. In light of this, Gauckler proposed in 1894 a classification for monuments of importance in Carthage, to provide protection for them. He identified several sites suitable for such a classification, including the ruins on the Byrsa hill, the Punic tombs, the cisterns, the Antonine Baths and the amphitheatre. Many of these were on land owned by the Church – as Freed notes, by 1892 nearly half of the ancient site had been purchased by the White Fathers.[24] As a result, the proposal met with great resistance from that body. In the end, only the Byrsa hill was classified along with Damous-el-Karita and Borjd Djedid in May 1895 (see Plans 1.1 and 1.2 in Chapter 1).

Despite the legislation that had been intended to provide a framework for the regulation of archaeology in Tunisia, excavations continued to be undertaken surreptitiously. In his role as director, there was a host of other diversions that took Gauckler away from his primary task of overseeing matters in the field. It is important to remember that the budget he had to work with was very small in comparison to the job at hand, since the remit for the Department of Antiquities included the entire country, and finds were continually being made. Exasperation is evident in several of his letters in this period. He was constantly having to deal with both Delattre and Carton, which began to have an effect on his health. He was also attacked in the papers in Tunisia – a development that Carton may have been behind.[25] Ultimately, Gauckler was forced to step down, with Alfred Merlin appointed as the new director of the Department of Antiquities in October 1905. It is not clear why it was felt necessary to remove Gauckler at this time, but he never held another post in Tunisia. He moved to Italy, where he would undertake further research until his death by suicide in December 1911.

In the final account, though, Gauckler along with Delattre undertook one of the most important projects for the future of the site. This was the creation of a topographic and archaeological plan of Carthage. Named after the engineer who oversaw the survey, the Bordy map was created in 1897. That Delattre was involved made much sense, given his knowledge of the ancient city. Not only does the map show the archaeological sites with great accuracy, it also indicates previous excavation trenches. It is likely that the end result was greatly influenced by what Gauckler and Delattre thought was important to illustrate, but even just carrying out such a survey was a monumental step forward for archaeology in Carthage. The Bordy map remains an essential resource for anyone interested in the topography and archaeology of ancient Carthage.[26]

7

The Tophet, Carthage and the Early Twentieth Century

Archaeology at Carthage took a back seat during the global turmoil of the First World War. Over 200,000 troops from the Mahgreb, both volunteers and conscripts, were recruited into European theatres of war over the course of 1914–18. It was after the war that the movement towards Tunisian independence gained strength on a national scale, with the foundation of the Destour (Constitution) party advocating for independence from France and political autonomy for the country.[1] Although the political and social landscape in Tunisia started to change in the post-First World War years, at Carthage archaeology was still firmly in the control of the colonial powers. There was, in fact, a tense atmosphere in the interwar period at the site. Official excavations were carried out under the auspices of the Department of Antiquities at the same time as the ever-present clerical archaeologists pressed on with their missions. The long-lived Delattre continued to excavate even though in his seventies, while increasingly present were teams of archaeologists from other countries engaged in research and projects inspired by popular media and an interest in all things ancient. In the midst of these efforts there was also a great deal of clandestine digging focused on finding and selling off artefacts.

A key catalyst for archaeological research in the 1920s was an explosion in urban development around Tunis and the whole peninsula. Tunis more than doubled in size in the first decades of the twentieth century, to the extent that the American archaeologist Francis Kelsey, working at the time, noted that 'the site of Carthage, once placed under a curse by its destroyers, is having a real-estate boom like that of an American or west-Canadian town'. Kelsey even published a realtor's map illustrating the subdivisions being sold off around the Roman theatre that had been excavated by Paul Gauckler at the turn of the century. Carthage had once again become a desirable place to live, out of the heat and humidity of Tunis and a place where 'fresh breezes blew off the sea'. Kelsey, an academic and excavator from the University of Michigan, was in many ways visionary in how he recognized the need to establish an archaeological park at the site to protect what still remained. His article, published in 1926, identified a conservation issue that would not be addressed for another fifty years through protective legislation.[2]

Kelsey was critical of the way that the French administration in Tunisia did not restrict development at Carthage to protect its heritage. He noted that in France, private real estate would not be allowed to be built on top of a site as important and unique as Carthage. By the 1920s, French heritage practice in France prohibited modern construction on ancient sites, and any building permits required official permission and survey. Very different rules applied to heritage in the colonial protectorate. Pivotal to the increased development in and around Carthage was the already mentioned commuter railway that had first been built in the nineteenth century and then updated with a tram line in 1907. Tunis was linked with nearby La Marsa (see Plan 5.1 in Chapter 5) so that by the 1920s, Carthage was one of the most desirable of the suburbs of Tunis. That development and construction at the site had destroyed much material evidence was recognized by many contemporaries.[3] Modern building development and land use would consistently remain a key part of the formation of the archaeological site at Carthage from the early twentieth century onwards.

There are times when the story of one particular archaeological site takes precedence over the different excavators who worked at Carthage, and the discovery of the place called the 'Tophet' in the early 1920s is one such time.[4] The construction boom of the postwar years led directly to the location of this most controversial and important archaeological site at Carthage. It is referred to as the Tophet of Salammbô, but often called the Precinct or Sanctuary of Tanit as well. The Tophet was one of few places with origins going back to the very foundations of the original Phoenician colony at Carthage and there is no other site that better reflects the popular attitudes towards Punic Carthage and its reception in the twentieth and into the twenty-first century. It is fair to say that the discovery of the Tophet caused an international stir.

The Tophet at Carthage resides in the Salammbô neighbourhood just to the north of the area known as the ancient commercial port (see Plan 1.1 in Chapter 1). The actual name Tophet has nothing to do with the archaeological space discovered at Carthage in the 1920s but originates from a number of passages in the Hebrew Bible that refer to an area known as *Tofet* (e.g., 2 Kings 26). Given that Tofet in the Hebrew Bible refers to a specific locality in the 'valley of Ben-hinnom' in Jerusalem, this is clearly a misnomer for the Carthaginian site. Nevertheless, the name has become synonymous with the space in Carthage. While we do not know what the Carthaginians themselves called this sacred precinct of their city, we do know it was dedicated to the goddess Tanit and her consort, Ba'al-Hammon. The area is sometimes referred to as the Sanctuary of Tanit or the Sanctuary of Ba'al but is still generally known by the biblical term and, for the sake of simplicity, we employ it here as well.

Rumours of the existence of a Tophet had been part of the grand narrative of the history of Punic Carthage since ancient times. In their references to the Carthaginian Tophet, both Greek and Roman sources made accusations of the sacrifice of children, with ancient writers such as Diodorus Siculus (20.14.4–7) and Plutarch (*De Superstitione* 13) providing graphic and imagined details. These references, which discuss how children were sacrificed to the god through the rite of fire, were often used to help magnify one of the many Roman stereotypes of their barbaric Carthaginian enemies. In fact, such a stereotype has persisted through to the twenty-first century, and in fictionalized accounts of ancient Carthage, the sacrifices are often recounted and embellished. Perhaps the most well-known of these is that created by Flaubert in his novel *Salammbô*. Written in the nineteenth century, well before the discovery of the Tophet, this piece of historical fiction was set just after the First Punic War (264–241 BCE), as we noted in Chapter 5. In his work, Flaubert boldly imagined a sacrificial area within ancient Carthage, making use of the descriptions in the ancient sources, especially that of Diodorus Siculus. Some fifty years after Flaubert, in the era of silent film, the Italian director Giovanni Pastroni created a popular visual image of human sacrifice at Carthage in the 1914 film, *Cabiria*. Pastroni chose the Second Punic War and the story of Hannibal as his backdrop. *Cabiria* was hugely influential and a global success, and its impact can be traced through motion picture history to the present day. This includes being the very first film ever projected at the White House in Washington when in June of 1914 an outdoor screening was held for President Woodrow Wilson, his cabinet and their wives.[5]

It was the discovery of one particular, now infamous, votive stele that ignited postwar interest in the area of the Tophet. The story reads a bit like a detective novel combined with aspects of the Keystone Cops. A stele was offered for sale on a December day in 1921 to a French man named Paul Gielly. It was an unusual piece. The stele had an incised design that showed a man in a robe striding forward with an infant curled in his left arm and the right arm stretched out before him (see Figure 7.1). As it happens, Gielly had some knowledge of the material culture at Carthage and was an amateur archaeologist whose day job was as a municipal tax collector with the French protectorate. He immediately recognized the unique nature of the incised stele and asked the vendor where he had found it. The seller was unwilling to give away his source and lied about the provenance of the piece. Gielly was unconvinced and spent some time following the man around Carthage. The seller ended up at a site located near the Punic ports in the neighbourhood now called Salammbô (see Plan 1.1 in Chapter 1).

Over the course of archaeological research at Carthage in the nineteenth century, the discovery of Punic stelae had hinted at the possibility of a sacred area, but the exact location was unknown. It is worth noting that the very first mention of the prospect of a sanctuary of this sort in a material way goes back a century to the Dutch engineer Jean-Emile Humbert. In 1817, after he uncovered four, in-situ, Punic votive stelae, he had suggested the possibility of

0   30cm   **FIGURE** 7.1 *The priest stele (drawn by Stephen Copp).*

an open-air sanctuary (see Figure 3.3 in Chapter 3). In fact, the traces of a sacred area dedicated to the Carthaginian goddess Tanit persistently excited excavators at Carthage looking for stele and inscriptions. Over the course of the nineteenth century, there were more stelae found and it is possible that some of those catalogued by Pricot de Sainte-Marie had originally come from the Tophet. There were also the notable excavations by two French archaeologists, Ernst Babelon and Solomon Reinach, in 1883 and the already mentioned doctor and archaeologist Louis Carton, who in 1916 had purchased some land that would later become incorporated into the site we know as the Tophet. Carton had done this in order to preserve the space from development.

Once Gielly had traced the origins of the infamous stele, he teamed up with his friend, François Icard, who was also the chief of police for Tunis, and arranged for the land to be bought. They then commenced excavation. This is a perfect example of how archaeology was conducted in the early 1920s at Carthage. The pair of colonial civil servants set to work as soon as they could and they dug in their off hours and on the weekends that Christmas time of 1921. The two men were amateurs and enthusiasts but also, to be fair, instrumental in saving the site from further destruction and despoliation due to clandestine excavations and development.

What was uncovered in those winter months of late 1921 and early 1922 was an open-air sanctuary that dated back to the very foundation of the Phoenician city of Carthage. It was a site that yielded a complex and densely occupied stratigraphy. The discoveries of that initial excavation were very much like those of all subsequent excavations that have since been held there, with work ongoing sporadically for the past century. Hundreds of limestone and sandstone stelae and cippi (architectural funerary monuments) were uncovered, along with ceramic funerary urns (see Figure 7.2). Inside these urns were the cremated remains of infants and sometimes animals. There was an enormous number of them. In fact, Icard noted that in one day he extracted 150 urns from the site. It was a complicated and intricate site and by February 1922, the Department of Antiquities at Carthage, led by Louis Poinssot at the time, had stepped in to take over the excavations. Since that very first discovery, work at the Tophet has been fraught with difficulty and, although a succession of excavations have been carried out, many questions still remain.[6] The site has only ever been partially excavated. The early excavations ran into problems and out of funds, while after the initial clamour and controversies of the discovery, there were disagreements between the Department of Antiquities and the owners of the land. The haul of stelae, cippi and urns from the first excavations were never properly recorded in situ and much of the information from these finds was lost.[7]

On the other hand, the excitement of the discovery of the stele and the detective work done to find its source led to the preservation of this important and essential site in the history of Punic Carthage. It would be difficult to overestimate the impact of locating the Tophet on the reputation of Carthage as an archaeological site. For example, in the 1922 issue of the

FIGURE 7.2 *The Tophet (photo by Sandra Bingham).*

Revue Tunisienne, there are four articles reporting on various aspects of the finds. Both the professional archaeologists and the amateurs who had been key to the discovery of the sanctuary were contributors. Charles Saumagne, the director of the *Revue Tunisienne*, wrote a foreword about the discoveries as well as an article on the finds. Icard and Gielly, the men who first uncovered the remains of the sanctuary, also published a paper. Paul Pallary wrote about the funerary urns, while Eusèbe Vassel published the votive inscriptions found on the stelae. There are many other publications on the Tophet in those early years of the 1920s by Louis Poinnsot and Raymond Lantier, who was inspector of the Antiquities of Tunisia from 1921 to 1926. There was also a surge of interest by the general public as articles appeared in the popular press about the site itself, with titles such as 'Gruesome Discovery in Ancient Carthage' (*The Times*, Monday, 14 August 1922).[8]

The very idea of a site where the sacrificed remains of children had been deposited was – and still is – shocking. For a world that had just fought the first ever world war and seen millions die, it almost came across as traumatic. There is a sense, in the popular reports of the finds, of a kind of eager sensationalism, an urge to look back and vilify an ancient society that seemed even more barbaric than the present day. This connection between past and present had already been clearly articulated in a review of the film *Cabiria* in the edition of *Punch* magazine for 15 April 1915 which stated that 'the ruthless methods of the Carthaginians twenty-two centuries ago – methods which have had to wait until the events if 1914–1915 to be equalled – were done in the name of their god Moloch'.[9] And this was before the actual discovery of the urns and stelae. The barbarity, death and slaughter of the First World War was embedded in the public imagination and it was easy, therefore, to connect it to the Tophet site at Carthage once it had been found. It seemed almost a confirmation of all that the ancient Roman stereotypes claimed of their old enemies, the Carthaginians. Current thinking and scholarship on the Tophet, on the other hand, is much more nuanced and less 'othering' of the Carthaginians in the broader context of contemporary societies, human sacrifice and the significance of the site as a foundational place in Carthaginian history. The last twenty years of scholarship and new excavations and interpretations have shifted focus toward understanding the significance of the site rather than accusing the Carthaginians of barbarity.[10]

Around the same time the Tophet was discovered, one of the more unusual characters in the story of the archaeology of Carthage entered the fray. He was 'Count' Byron Khun de Prorok, a Mexican-born American citizen of Hungarian descent, author of *Digging for Lost African Gods* and shameless self-promoter. De Prorok visited Carthage in the early 1920s and, once Icard's excavations had been stopped by the Department of Antiquities, he bought part of the land that had preserved the Tophet. The dashing de Prorok fit the mould of the romantic archaeological adventurer and he was inspired by the finds, by the urns filled with the remains of young children, animals and burnt offerings and by the stories told of sacrifices to the ancient gods. His plan was to pursue further research on the land he had purchased. As with all archaeological excavations, funding was the first priority, so de Prorok set off to convince an American public that the site of Carthage was at risk and to garner support for new excavations. What de Prorok lacked in facts and details about Carthage, he made up for in panache, style and presentation. His tour of the United States in 1922 attracted a great deal of publicity for Carthage as an archaeological site and as one of the great ancient cities. De Prorok's reputation as a public speaker was prodigious even if his work as an archaeologist was often derided.[11] By working hard at both publicizing the site and at self-promotion, along with stirring up a sense of the threat to Carthage by increased urban development, he was instrumental in the formation of a Franco-American project at Carthage in 1925 that had the Tophet at its heart.

De Prorok is a fascinating character in so many ways. He is easy to dismiss because of his character, a kind of proto-Indiana Jones, even though he was quite innovative in his approach to archaeology. He applied up-to-date technology to the excavations at Carthage for the first time when he used the new motion picture technology.[12] This he employed to showcase the excavations in his presentations about Carthage that thrilled audiences across North America and Europe. As noted in a *New York Times* magazine article of 14 January 1923, the dashing figure, along with archaeology and romance, all came together with technology to showcase what could be done at the site. Sadly, all the films that captured the state of Carthage in his day are lost.

De Prorok writes in his book that they were inspired to film what was going on in the field but notes that not everyone greeted the new technology and methodology with enthusiasm. There are still photographs that record some of the events described and show the young handsome de Prorok with various key players in the archaeological landscape of Carthage at the time, including the venerable Delattre (see Figure 7.3). We also see evidence of his team in action, filming the cleaning of a spectacular Roman mosaic at an unknown location (see Figure 7.4). It is not hard to imagine that the film technology must have been quite a curiosity for Delattre who was then in his seventies and who had a starring role in the productions. We are not sure of the Church's official reaction to the films and perhaps it is they who were the sceptics that de Prorok mentions. In any event, De Prorok's role was significant enough for Kelsey to dedicate his 1926 publication on the excavations at Carthage to him, but it is widely assumed that de Prorok needed to bring in a scholar of Kelsey's credibility to enhance his own standing.

De Prorok had many other interests of note and was also involved in early attempts at aerial photography and filming for archaeological research at Carthage. To do this he teamed up with the photographer Robert Alexander MacLean and a motion picture expert, Prince Edgard de Waldeck, and they took to the skies to image the site from above for the very first time. The cast of characters involved is fascinating and elusive, as exemplified by the Scottish-Canadian MacLean. He had enlisted with the Winnipeg Grenadiers in 1914 but worked as an intelligence officer with the British Army in the Middle East. Very little can be pieced together of his activities

FIGURE 7.3 *At the Tophet: de Prorok is third from the left, Delattre on the far right, with Kelsey second right (courtesy of the Kelsey Museum of Archaeology).*

FIGURE 7.4 *De Prorok filming the cleaning of a mosaic at Carthage* (© *Royal Geographic Society*).

during the war, but when he arrived in Carthage, he was fresh from early aerial photography at archaeological sites in what was then the British protectorate of Transjordan and Iraq. MacLean was not the first cross-over between spy and archaeologist and it is notable that his ideas and skills helped to bring to fruition many of de Prorok's interests and questions about the site of Carthage. The men photographed and filmed over the coastline and the ports in Punic Carthage, and over a wide area of the peninsula from La Goulette to Cap Gammarth (see Map 1.2 in Chapter 1).[13]

While nothing of de Prorok's films survive, we do have photo stills of some of the aerial flights that show he was interested in the coastal areas and landscape of the peninsula (see Figure 7.5). The description of what was visible from the air at the site of Carthage provides mouth-watering details for those interested in the topography of the city before it was covered by modern suburban houses. Yet the gallant and dapper de Prorok is often written off entirely because of the quality of his publications. Of his main book, *Digging for Lost African Gods*, a contemporary reviewer in the 1926 volume of the *American Journal of Archaeology* notes that 'for the dilettante, who may have before him an idle two hours and no particular desire for either much or accurate information, the work is to be recommended'.[14] Ouch.

The Tophet continued to be the focus of excavations at Carthage throughout the 1920s and 1930s. Of note were the excavations by Francis

FIGURE 7.5 *Aerial photo of the cathedral and Carthage Museum (© Royal Geographic Society).*

Kelsey and the young Scottish archaeologist Donald B. Harden in 1924 and 1925. Their work added a great deal to our understanding and to the approaches to interpreting the Tophet as a site. One of the most significant advancements in the knowledge and understanding came in the form of a detailed stratigraphic plan that attempted to break down the use of the site into chronological phases. These phases are often still referred to today as Tanit I, II and III (see Figure 7.6). Kelsey and Harden only managed to excavate for one season at the Tophet. Though funding was available, it seems that Kelsey was reluctant to accede to the demands that had been made by Poinssot, the Director of Antiquities, and he continued to believe that only large-scale excavations would do justice to such an important site. Further work was done at the Tophet by the successor to Delattre, Gabriel-Guillaume Lapeyre, on the land purchased by Louis Carton in the 1930s, but it is much less well regarded. These excavations continued to amass an enormous amount of material from the site, thousands of urns, stele and cippi. In fact, the excavation records by Lapeyre state that they uncovered 2,000 ex-voto inscriptions alone, but although all this material was collected, it was never properly published.[15]

There was a great deal of excavation at Carthage in the interwar period that often gets overlooked because of the scope, importance and controversial nature of the finds at the Tophet. A good example are the excavations and published work of Charles Saumagne. He was a prolific excavator at Carthage, another who came to archaeology as a hobby, having originally trained as a lawyer and whose day job from 1924 was to head up the

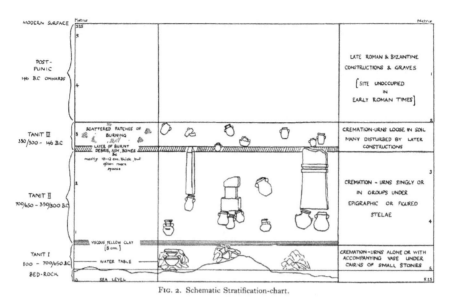

FIG. 2. Schematic Stratification-chart.

FIGURE 7.6 *Stratigraphy of the Tophet by Harden (Iraq, 1937).*

Tunisian civil service. Saumagne would go on to excavate and publish during the 1920s and 1930s on many of the vexing questions about the history of Carthage, all of this in parallel with fulfilling his role as chief civil servant. His published work considered the location of the Punic ports, the topography of the city and the position of the original Roman colony of Gaius Gracchus, among broader ideas. Saumagne's excavations on the Byrsa hill during the interwar years sought to establish what, if anything, could still be traced of the original Punic settlements and how the Roman city fit on top of it. The city of Carthage was very much in his blood, with his parents living in a house on the slopes of the Byrsa hill and much of his excavation there focused on the northeast corner of the hill owned by his family. A talented archaeologist, Saumagne's methodical and measured approach to the places he excavated means that much of what he recorded still holds great value today.

Partially as a result of the unrestrained development and increased archaeological activities in the 1920s and the attention that the discoveries at the Tophet garnered, there was a more pressing interest in imposing some sort of regulation and control on archaeological research at Carthage. The idea of protecting the archaeological remains at the site had been suggested for quite some time as we have discussed, but in the 1920s there were many different voices who supported an attempt at further site conservation. Kelsey and Carton had both advocated more restriction on development, and Poinssot, during his tenure as the Director of Antiquities, attempted to establish a kind of protected zone that encompassed key areas in the later 1920s. Poinssot, however, was not a popular figure and his manner seems to have made him many enemies, in particular Carton, who eviscerated the director in various letters and publications. Unrest among those responsible for the site of Carthage in this period is perhaps reflective of the insecurities of a colonial elite in the face of growing calls for independence in the Tunisian population. In the early 1920s the pressure was intense enough for the French government to send the illustrious historian Stéphane Gsell to Carthage to evaluate the situation in 1924. A final proposal for an archaeological park was made to the French government and Poinssot's letter outlining the plan can be examined in the 1928–9 edition of the prestigious *Bulletin Archéologique du Comité des travaux historique et scientifique* (Archaeological Bulletin of the Committee of Historical and Scientific Works). This attempt to make Carthage an 'historic zone' ultimately failed, with the result that the site would continue to be preserved in a piecemeal fashion dependent on the intentions of those who owned the land.[16]

The interests of the Catholic Church at Carthage were still an ongoing and important factor in how the ancient site was regarded. This can be best viewed through the lens of the Eucharistic Congress of 1930. Carthage was the location of this gathering of members of the Catholic community, including clergy and lay people, which was held in celebration and reaffirmation of the role of the Eucharist in the Catholic faith. The first Eucharistic Congress had been held in 1881 and the choice of Carthage as the location of the Thirtieth Congress was significant in many ways. It would be the first time the congress was held in Africa, and ancient Carthage's association with early Christianity was a driving force behind the selection. The message of the Catholic Church in North Africa as an extension of French colonial aspirations underpinned much of this event. The year 1930 also marked, not coincidentally, the centenary of France's takeover of Algeria, an event that was often celebrated as the re-establishment of the Catholic Church in North Africa, linking ancient Christian traditions with colonial power.

The congress attracted an international crowd, with several thousand people in attendance. The focus was not only the Eucharist in the Catholic faith but also the archaeology of Carthage. For the eighty-year-old Delattre, who would die not long afterwards (in January 1932), the congress provided the perfect opportunity to showcase his faith as well as his role as an archaeologist over the past decades. These two deeply intertwined aspects of his life and career would leave a lasting impact on the modern world's interpretations of Delattre's work at ancient Carthage. The congress certainly put the ancient site on display. A few details of the key events are enough to get the flavour and intention of the gathering. It took place over several days and many sites of the ancient city, including the amphitheatre, Basilica Maiorum and the Basilica of St Cyprian, held pride of place (see Plan 1.2 in Chapter 1). Records show that all of these sites had been the target of various reconstruction efforts in the years leading up to the congress in order to highlight the importance of the ruins and reinforcing their underpinning of the events taking place. On the final day of the congress, there was a procession from the amphitheatre to the Cathedral of St Louis on the Byrsa hill (see Plan 1.2 in Chapter 1). There was also a parade, consisting of children dressed as crusaders, that wound through the site and ended in the amphitheatre. This is perhaps the most disconcerting part of the entire congress from a modern perspective, only emphasized by the fact that the parade took place on 10 May 1930 which happened to coincide with Eid-al-Fitr, one of the most holy of days in the Muslim religious calendar.[17]

Looking at the Eucharistic Congress from the vantagepoint of almost a century later, it seems that there was an astounding arrogance and insensitivity in the blatant demonstration of the Christian faith and crusading narrative in a state where the majority of the population were Muslim. Yet this was the design: to emphasize or perhaps reinforce the underlying power of the Church and the protectorate in a period of political turmoil and rising calls for independence. Such an overt message as presented by the congress was, not surprisingly, greeted with extreme hostility and derision by most Tunisians. In fact, the Eucharistic Congress of 1930 served as a direct catalyst for many Tunisian political activists and artists. The Tunisian poet and writer Ali Al-Du'aji was directly inspired by the congress to focus his output on a new Tunisian cultural expression. The movement that emerged presented a new voice and vision in art and literature that was rooted in North African culture and the Mediterranean. On the political front, the congress was key in inspiring a young twenty-seven-year-old man named Habib Bourguiba. Bourguiba, born in the coastal city of Monastir, would become a leading voice in Tunisian independence and, eventually, the country's first president.[18]

Archaeology in the 1930s continued apace but was largely put on hold with the advent of the Second World War. The political situation in Tunisia at the start of the war was complex. The Pétain government in France was nominally ruling through the protectorate, with the Tunisian Moncef Bey of the Husainid dynasty holding court at his palace in La Marsa. This resulted in pressure coming from all sides. Tunisia became a major theatre of war, especially from November 1942 with the arrival of Axis troops through to the end of their occupation in May 1943. The impact on the local population has not always been emphasized in narratives of the great battles fought across North Africa between the British Eighth Army and the German Afrika Korps commanded by Field Marshal Erwin Rommel. It makes sobering reading to consider the devastation to both the population and the landscape of much of Tunisia and its cities in this period. Tunisians suffered enormous hardships under Italian and German occupation and then massive destruction in the bombing campaign to liberate the region by the Allied forces. Although Tunis and Carthage were relatively untouched, the port at La Goulette was heavily damaged and massive destruction was wrought on coastal cities like Sfax and Bizerte. The impact of the chaos and turmoil would take many years to recover from. During the years of fighting, it is estimated that up to 35 per cent of the population were starving and much of the country's existing infrastructure destroyed.[19]

With this backdrop, the site of Carthage once again played a part in the propaganda and ideology of a broader geopolitical conflict. This time it wasn't the Holy Roman Emperor or the Ottoman Sultan vying for control of the strategic region and riding out to ancient Carthage to emphasize their credentials, but the Axis and Allied forces. When Winston Churchill made a secret visit in June of 1943, just a month after Tunisia had been liberated, he did so to address British troops who had massed in Carthage. The publicity for the tour featured the ruins at the site, which was a key feature of the media coverage. There are evocative scenes with Churchill addressing the troops who line the *cavea* (seats) of the Roman theatre at Carthage (see Chapter 6, Figure 6.5; it is worth noting that, on the original images, the location is often incorrectly identified as the amphitheatre).

Despite the chaos and upheaval of the war and its aftermath, however, some excavations continued at Carthage from 1944 through to 1947. Pierre Cintas, for example, excavated during that period at the Tophet, making some key observations on the structures related to the sanctuary. The *Chapelle Cintas* is used to refer to a building that was intricately related to the sanctuary site but whose function has long been debated. In other locations at the ancient site, we can see that excavations started again and that in many cases finds were being recorded in an ad hoc manner. There is notice that, in December of 1945, forty German prisoners of war (still in Tunisia at this point after the official end of war) were set to clear the ruins of the site of the Antonine Baths. This work was begun under the direction of Gilbert-Charles Picard, director of the Department of Antiquities in Tunisia from 1942 to 1955, who would continue to study the vast imperial baths for almost a decade. The baths, which had been a point of interest in the mid-nineteenth century for the British consul Thomas Reade (see Chapter 3), had never been systematically excavated and recorded. They were largely uncovered in this immediate postwar period and the ruins of the baths remain some of the showpiece sites of the archaeological park at Carthage (see Figure 1.3 in Chapter 1).[20]

The early twentieth century was a key transitional period for Carthage as an archaeological site and neighbourhood in a world that had seen massive social, political and economic change. The way that Carthage, as a place, had been claimed as a key part of colonial and Christian narratives by the European powers in North Africa would, for the first time, be challenged in the post-Second World War period. The rise of Tunisia as an independent nation would lead to a new phase of interaction between the landscape of Carthage, its heritage and the political atmosphere surrounding it. This took place in the midst of continued urbanization, rising political awareness, shifting identities and archaeological excavation at the site.

8

Independence, UNESCO and the Twenty-First Century

When independence from France was finally achieved in 1956, the first president of a sovereign Tunisia would be Habib Bourguiba, the very man for whom the Eucharistic Congress at Carthage in 1930 had served as a catalyst. Bourguiba had spent much of the intervening twenty-five years leading a popular nationalist movement and doing all he could to promote the cause of independence, which also began to be advanced by trade unions in Tunisia following the Second World War. By the early 1950s, the process of decolonization and the collapse of European empires that had begun soon after 1945 was in full swing in Asia and across Africa. In North Africa specifically, Libya would be the first country to become an independent nation, with the Kingdom of Libya being established in 1951. A war of independence – a bloody and brutal conflict – was fought in Algeria from 1954 to 1962. In Tunisia, attempts were made to find a way that would accommodate both French interests and Tunisian authority. It was not easy going, with rival factions in Tunisia holding quite different views on how to achieve their goals. The French government proved reluctant to let go of the protectorate and Bourguiba was imprisoned and exiled in 1954, the same year that war broke out in Algeria. But with the situation in Tunisia growing increasingly unstable and France fighting a war in her neighbouring country, the decision was made to allow Bourguiba to return the following year. He landed, triumphantly, to cheering crowds at La Goulette in June of 1955 (see Figure 8.1). Bourguiba would play a key role in the negotiations that followed in that same year. At first, only limited autonomy was granted to Tunisia, but in March 1956 the end of the protectorate was announced and Tunisia finally earned its independence and was recognized by France.[1]

The decade between the end of the Second World War and independence was one of rebuilding after the damage caused by the war. As a result, archaeology often had to take a back seat to urban development. Nowhere was that more evident than in Carthage. Some excavation continued in this period, in particular, at the Tophet under Cintas (as mentioned in Chapter 7); on the Byrsa hill under Colette Picard (1947) and Jean Ferron and Maurice Pinard (1953–4); and at the Antonine Baths by Gilbert-Charles

FIGURE 8.1 *The return of Habib Bourguiba from exile in 1955 (© Getty).*

Picard and others (1946–57).[2] In 1953, under the direction of Colette Picard, who was then curator of the Carthage site, the Antonine Baths and environs were finally designated an archaeological park. It had taken nearly thirty years since the official proposal had been made by Gsell, and although the space was on a much smaller scale than had first been envisioned, it was at least a first step.

Bourguiba was president of Tunisia for thirty years (1957–87). He believed passionately in a programme of modernization for Tunisia and achieved much in the early part of his tenure. Archaeology, in the midst of all of the other issues the country was facing, was not a high priority. The fate of Carthage in the late 1950s and early 1960s shows the danger that modernization can bring to an archaeological site. Always a desirable place to live, Carthage again became a building site. Coupled with the reforestation of the area and road improvements, the archaeological site was at great risk. One of the key elements that contributed to this threat was the decision by Bourguiba to build his new presidential palace at Carthage. This prestigious construction began in the late 1950s and would continue until 1969. The resulting substantial palace and building complex brought about a huge change to the area of the sea front of Carthage. The location could not have been more perfect for a palace. It was in a prime area right next to the sea, on the hill of Sainte-Monique, overlooking the magnificent Antonine Baths (see Plan 5.1 in Chapter 5). On this very same spot, Mustapha Khasnadar, first minister of the bey in the third quarter of the eighteenth century, had also built his villa. The hill was also the site of a significant Punic-era necropolis excavated by Delattre, where the two marble anthropoid sarcophagi had been discovered (see Figure 6.3 in Chapter 6). Any residual archaeology that had remained by the time of the Bourguiba building project, however, was lost as access to the location was highly regulated. Naturally, the president's choice of residence resulted in many other impressive houses being built nearby for the elite of the Tunisian government and ministers, with foreign embassies soon moving to the area as well. Carthage and the neighbourhoods around it had once again become the seat of power in the country.

It is thought that, by situating his palace at Carthage, Bourguiba may have been associating the new country with its ancient heritage and its venerable past. It is almost as if he was capturing Carthage and all it stood for. It would not be until 1964, however, that the buildings owned by the Catholic Church on the Byrsa hill, and in particular the Cathedral of St Louis and the Museum, were officially returned to the State. It is perhaps from that moment that interest in ancient Carthage began to grow more broadly among the Tunisian population. The complexity of the cultural heritage of ancient Carthage in its many guises, in a newly independent Arab state, cannot be underestimated. Independence had happened relatively quickly and the population of Tunisia was – and is – of very mixed origins. The majority of Tunisians are of Amazigh ethnicity (more than 60 per cent of the population), with Arab, African and European populations mixed in. They are mostly Muslim but include Jewish and Christian regional populations as well. Up until this point, ancient Carthage had largely been viewed as a place of European cultural interests, with its emphasis on Roman imperial power and Christian traditions. This was especially true throughout the period of the protectorate, when the French government and the White Fathers had used these links for the purposes of politics, religion and power.

As a result, the general population of Tunisia was somewhat detached from the archaeology of Carthage. In his recent book on the site, Ennabli suggests that it was ignored because educated Tunisians were not aware of the riches that Carthage had to offer. These treasures had been kept at a distance during the monopoly on excavations by the European archaeologists and the Catholic Church in the century before independence.[3] It is also the case that there were other pasts that were important to the population of the new state, including Arab Islamic, Amazigh and Jewish histories and traditions. That is, the history of Punic, Roman and Christian Carthage had been separated off from Tunisian cultural memory and so the threat to the archaeological heritage of Carthage once independence had been achieved took some time to be fully recognized.

Key to the preservation of the remains at Carthage was a restriction placed on building inside the archaeological zone. The urgency was laid out in an article in the *UNESCO Courier* of December 1970, where it was predicted that if no action was taken, the site would be completely destroyed by 1985.[4] Tunis was undergoing rapid growth and the need for housing meant that encroachment on Carthage was inevitable. It was necessary, therefore, to balance two competing needs: ensuring that the archaeological site was protected while still providing controlled development. For Tunisian governmental authorities, the preservation of the cultural heritage of Carthage would also bring an economic benefit in the form of increased tourism. In the late 1960s, a plan was conceived to try to achieve these goals. The practicalities of enacting such a project were daunting enough, along with the vast expense of funding historical preservation and excavation at the level that was necessary. As a result, the decision was taken to ask for assistance from UNESCO. An initial study (the 'Tunis–Carthage Project', with 'Tunis' referring specifically to the Medina, the old city centre) was undertaken from 1969 to 1972. Recommendations in the report included the steps that should be taken at Carthage to preserve the remains, including the concept of an archaeological park. The report also advised on how best to facilitate new excavations. Yet it was acknowledged that accommodation had to be made not only for the archaeological site but equally for the requirements of those who lived in the area and for those who visited. The financing of such a wide-ranging project was impossible for the Tunisian government on its own and so funding was sought from international partners. Contributors included UNESCO alongside countries such as France, Germany and Canada.

On 19 May 1972, the 'Save Carthage' project (Campagne international de sauvegarde de Carthage) was initiated.[5] It would run until 1992 and, indeed, in various guises even into the early part of the twenty-first century. The aims were twofold: first, to try to save what was left at the site of Carthage from urban growth; and second, to preserve and restore remains that had already been uncovered. Under the banner of UNESCO, teams of archaeologists from many nations in Europe, Asia and North America, working with Tunisian authorities and archaeologists, were involved in a concerted effort to further unravel the archaeological potential at Carthage. The work was initially overseen by the INAA (Institut National d'Archeologie et d'Art), later to become the INP (Institut National du Patrimoine/National Heritage Institute). Abdelmajid Ennabli became the curator of the site and served as the director of the National Museum of Carthage from 1973 to 2001. He would play a major role throughout the UNESCO project. The international body was also involved in the creation of a document centre called CEDAC (Centre d'étude et de documentation archéologique de la conservation de Carthage/Centre of Archaeological Study and Documentation of the Conservation of Carthage), which was part of the Tunisian Institute of Archaeology. A bulletin was published twice a year (later annually) that focused on dissemination of the results of the ongoing UNESCO projects and other connected research at the site.

What distinguished the UNESCO project from earlier excavations at Carthage was that, for the first time, there was a common goal: to work together to significantly improve knowledge of the interconnected histories and heritage of the Punic, Roman and late antique city. The involvement of so many teams meant that excavation could be carried out on a large scale. This was the realization of what Charles Beulé had pointed out in the mid-nineteenth century and what had been hinted at by Kelsey in the early twentieth century: that the potential of the site would only be achieved by having the means – both in terms of manpower and finance – to excavate systematically. A monograph published in 1992, consisting of twenty-nine papers and edited by Ennabli, *Pour sauver Carthage* (*To Save Carthage*), provides a contemporary idea of the scope and importance of the excavations undertaken during the campaign at key sites in the ancient city.[6]

Many countries took part in the project, including Germany whose excavations of the Quartier Magon and exploration of the layout of the Punic city have been influential in our understanding of the early phase of occupation. American excavators focused on the Roman circus and Christian basilicas, while Canadians concentrated on the Roman odeon building and the line of the late antique Theodosian wall (see Plan 1.2 in Chapter 1). French teams excavated on the Byrsa hill, continuing the tradition begun by Beulé, examining both Punic and Roman remains there. Among the French archaeologists working on the Byrsa hill in the 1970s was Serge Lancel, who published not only excavation reports but also history, and his books on *Carthage*, *Hannibal* and *St. Augustine* remain influential.[7] Some of the most significant excavations carried out under the UNESCO banner was at two major Punic sites: at the ports by a British team led by Henry Hurst and at the Tophet by the American team under the direction of Lawrence Stager. Excavation at the iconic ports revealed that their date of construction was much later than had been previously thought: that is, they date to the period just after the Second Punic War (218–201 BCE). This considerably changed the way that the post Punic war period at Carthage was viewed in an historical sense. The study by Stager at the Tophet was instrumental in determining different phases of burial and in placing the site within its broader context in the wider Mediterranean. Hurst also contributed to our understanding of the Tophet by proving that the location was transformed in the Roman period, becoming a religious area with temples to Caelestis and Saturn, the Roman equivalents of the Carthaginian deities Tanit and Ba'al, although there remains, as with so many of the Carthaginian sites, some disagreement among scholars on this interpretation.

During the 'Save Carthage' campaign, as the site began to take on a greater significance because of what was being uncovered – and with a growing body of scholarship and international importance as a result – rules were tightened further regarding building in the area. This was aided by the fact that Carthage was declared a World Heritage Site by UNESCO in 1979. At the same time, the international body recommended the establishment of a National Archaeological Park at Carthage and also at the town of Sidi Bou Said, just north of Carthage (see Map 1.1 in Chapter 1). The park would encompass 500 hectares of the archaeological zone. In

1985, the Tunisian government recognized the site of Carthage in law – with zones designated *non aedificandi* (not to be built on) – and indicated its intention to establish the park. With international attention now focused on the site, it was hoped that the threat to the archaeology had been averted.

In 1987, Zine al-Abidine Ben Ali came to power in a coup. Bourguiba was declared unfit to rule and, after dominating political life in Tunisia for almost fifty years, he lived the rest of his life under house arrest (he died in 2000). The new regime expressed support for the preservation of Carthage and took an interest in the archaeological park, with the president directly involved in discussions about its establishment in 1991. Part of the reason, no doubt, was an interest in increasing tourism to the area, with the economic benefits that this would provide. A 'Heritage Code' for Tunisia was enacted in 1994, which allowed for fines and a prison sentence to be imposed on anyone who built in an archaeological zone. In the late 1990s, the park boundaries were defined (1996) and a Plan de Protection et de Mise en Valeur du Site de Carthage–Sidi Bou Said (PPMV, Plan for the Protection and Promotion of Carthage–Sidi Bou Said) was developed (1998). Meanwhile excavations continued in Carthage, with the Tunisian authorities and international community driving the work at the site.

But alongside these conservation-focused endeavours, there were worrying signs. The establishment of the archaeological park, with work expected to begin in 2001, was delayed by controversy and cost. Land that had been designated for protection was reclassified and building permitted, with the most heavily developed area that around the Punic ports (see Figure 8.2). UNESCO was sufficiently concerned about the ongoing construction that they intervened in 1995 and 1999, but without results. In fact, what was actually happening at Carthage when Ben Ali was president only became apparent after he was removed from power in 2011. It has subsequently come to light that he openly supported the proposals for preserving the archaeological heritage at Carthage while at the same time covertly thwarting them, often to the benefit of his own family and supporters. In the end, perhaps nothing reveals the attitude of his regime to the ancient site of Carthage more than the construction of the El Abidine Mosque (now Malik ibn Anas Mosque), completed in 2003 (see Figure 8.3). Its location, on the Odeon hill and close to Damous-el-Karita, one of the most significant sites of ancient Christian Carthage, seems visibly intended to provide a counterpoint to the Cathedral of St Louis (by that time deconsecrated and established as the Acropolium, an arts centre). The sheer size of the new construction, along with its vast parking lot and the construction of a path leading directly to the presidential palace, will have done untold damage to the archaeology.

The question must be asked, then: to what extent was the 'Save Carthage' project successful? On the plus side, it allowed extensive investigations into many of the most important sites in the ancient city, including the Byrsa hill, the Punic ports, the Punic cemeteries and the Tophet as well as the theatre,

FIGURE 8.2 *Modern view from the ports to the Byrsa hill (photo by Eve MacDonald).*

FIGURE 8.3 *Malik ibn Anas (formerly El Abidine) Mosque in Carthage (photo by Sandra Bingham).*

amphitheatre, circus, basilicas and the Antonine Baths. But the site also suffered, especially in the period when Ben Ali was in power. That he had allowed building to occur in Carthage in those areas that had been designated *non aedificandi* had not gone unnoticed, but there was little anyone could do. This is clear from UNESCO's attempts in the late 1990s to convince the president to adhere to the regulations concerning heritage sites. Efforts continued into the early part of this century, in particular to have the boundary of the archaeological site made clear and to ensure that development did not compromise its integrity.[8]

Tunisia ignited the spark that set off what was called the Arab Spring. Ben Ali was overthrown in January of 2011 and, in the aftermath of the revolution, concern over Carthage was voiced almost immediately. Ennabli once again was a key player along with a group called Les Amis de Carthage (The Friends of Carthage).[9] In March of that year, it was announced that the provisional government had passed a decree to reverse the changes in classification at the site that had taken place from 1992 to 2008, and a map was presented to UNESCO's World Heritage Centre that showed the boundaries of the archaeological park. In the following years, although some progress has been made (in particular, in updating the 1998 protection plan, the PPMV), very little actually took place on the ground as noted in the biannual (occasionally annual) reports on Carthage by the World Heritage Centre. Concerns about the site were mainly associated with illegal construction, the absence of legal oversight and the lack of a management plan.[10] The complexities resulting from a succession of new governments attempting to manage decades of corruption and mismanagement, alongside a severe lack of funds and disagreement among various participants and stakeholders, have made progress slow.

In late February 2019, more serious concerns were expressed about the amount of building taking place near the Roman circus in particular. Because of the continued building on the site and the slow removal of illegal structures, UNESCO officially informed the head of government that Carthage might be placed on the 'List of World Heritage in Danger'. Tunisian authorities met in March of that year and agreed that they would adhere to the recommendations made by the World Heritage Centre and ICOMOS (the International Council on Monuments and Sites). At that point, it was also noted that the circular harbour was being used illegally by fishing boats and that the protection plan (PPMV) had not yet been put in place. In the report presented in 2021, UNESCO offered some optimism and acknowledged the removal of many illegal buildings along with the purchasing of land in an attempt to control development. The most recent report (2023) indicates that illegal buildings continue to be demolished and that there has been movement on the integration of the archaeological park into the PPMV. There has also been further work on development strategies for research and conservation, including plans for construction of a new museum for Carthage on the Byrsa hill. Yet it also notes the need to be mindful of local residents and, in particular, to engage with them in any future plans for the site.[11] A recent scholarly study considered the attitude of Carthage residents towards supporting sustainable heritage tourism and found that, among those taking part in the survey, there was interest in being involved in decisions to protect the site.[12] The importance of including individuals from across society has been highlighted although the difficulty of doing this, given the somewhat challenging relationship between the government and those living in and around the area, was also noted by the report's authors. The neighbourhood's current residents are engaging with public heritage professionals, government directives and archaeological excavations in this new chapter in the ongoing story of Carthage.

9

Epilogue

Continuing Carthage

The dialogue and debate around how the Tunisian government and local population and neighbouring residents will investigate, conserve and present Carthage is an ongoing story. The history of archaeology at the site is complex and if this book has revealed anything, it is that Carthage has been buffeted by many and varied interests throughout the centuries. First Arabic and then European travellers visited, for curiosity and scholarly investigation. After the travellers came those who wanted to explore the ancient city. Many were disappointed with the remains they found at one of the most important cities of the ancient world. With the arrival of the earliest archaeologists (using that term loosely), we see the beginning of an understanding of the area of Carthage as an ancient landscape. Even when the techniques were rudimentary and the objectives questionable, the fact that we know so much about ancient Carthage in all its guises is a testament to those who took the time and effort to explore the site. It also attests to the lure of Carthage, something that continues today.

Archaeology also is constantly changing. Unlike the early explorers and excavators in these chapters, today's teams are engaged as much in science as in digging. We want to end with two observations by way of example. Science is certainly taking centre-stage with the material from the Tophet. The controversial nature of the remains has been the subject of impassioned discussion and there have been many emotive statements published by researchers of the site. For example, on its first discovery, the initial reaction was about a reinforcement of stereotyping and of 'othering' the Punic citizens of Carthage. Even now, every few years a story in the popular press appears about Carthaginian child sacrifice – or the denial of it. The ways in which the Tophet has been portrayed in the various periods during which excavations have taken place can often be seen as a bellwether for a larger role that Carthage is playing in internal politics, as heritage and patrimony are debated and crafted for different leaders. The approaches by the local tourist industry and the wider academic community have not always coalesced.

But the first twenty years of this century have been key in shifting the rhetoric about the Tophet away from moral judgement to the investigation of meaning and identity in the multicultural Mediterranean and colonial foundation that was ancient Carthage. Instrumental in this development was the publication in 2004 of Hélène Bénichou-Safar's *Le Tophet de Salammbô à Carthage: Essai de Reconstitution* (The Tophet of Salammbô in Carthage: An Attempt at Reconstruction). The work includes an in-depth look at the excavations, from Icard's first discoveries to the early twenty-first century, alongside the various finds. It also considers the state of the site. Bénichou-Safar collated and presented all the available evidence in order to better interpret the religious practices of the Carthaginians. Her approach without judgement provided a way forward with the Tophet. There are some things that are clear. The stelae are all quite uniform. The dedication has been set up in fulfilment of a vow and the god has been repaid for the granting of a wish. The remains are mostly very young infants and the site was of the utmost importance and sanctity to the ancient Carthaginians. The identity of the place and the importance of the sacrifices must be emphasized. Recent excavations led by Imed Ben Jerbania are changing our understanding of the stratigraphy, narrowing the dating, and have turned to using the latest scientific analysis on the bones to determine the exact age of the infants although, even here, debate continues. There are now many different routes available to continue the discussion of this important and controversial place.[1]

Another good example of where archaeology at Carthage sits today is the site of Bir Massouda (see Plan 1.1 in Chapter 1) – a place first explored in the late nineteenth century by Pricot de Sainte-Marie and then later by Salomon Reinach and Ernest Babelon, who published their findings in 1884. During the UNESCO project, part of the area was excavated by German and Dutch teams (1986–95) as well as those from Tunisia. In the early part of this century, scholars from Tunisia, Britain, the Netherlands and Belgium carried out a further series of rescue excavations at Bir Massouda when the site was about to be developed (a decision later overturned). The publications on the site highlight all that current archaeological techniques have to offer.[2] They reveal a place with a long occupation, from early in the Punic period to the Middle Ages. The excavations have clarified the topography of the archaic Punic city, including the city boundary. There is also evidence of the earliest necropolis (eighth century BCE) and an industrial zone, with metal-working taking place. Analysis has shown that this was at a large scale and from a very early period (sixth to fifth centuries BCE), with advanced skills for the time. That area was gradually transformed into a residential section as the city grew. Excavations in the northwest part of the site revealed Roman housing of mid-second century CE date, some of which also had commercial functions and shops attached, in multifunctional neighbourhoods.

This residential area remained in use until the sixth century when a sizeable basilica was built. Bir Massouda thus represents the full richness of archaeology at Carthage in the modern era and the publications are a testament to what meticulous excavation can reveal.

As we have shown through this examination of the individuals who played a part in the story of the archaeological history at Carthage, it was the Punic city that was often of greatest interest to the characters involved, followed closely by the Christian city. Interest in the former was mainly due to the novelty of Punic culture, as seen, for example, in the desire of Reuvens to acquire materials for the Dutch Archaeological Museum and by Davis and Pricot de Sainte Marie who enriched the British Museum and the Louvre. Christian Carthage was unsurprisingly the focus for the White Fathers, whose objectives were driven not only by a desire to uncover the past but to then employ this past as a way to promote their agenda in the contemporary environment. Roman Carthage, on the other hand, seemed to be less attractive to those exploring the site in the nineteenth century, although that phase of the city provides us with many important monuments such as the Antonine Baths, the odeon and the theatre. Even today, when looking for comprehensive studies on the ancient city, it is easier to find materials on Punic and on Christian Carthage. For example, Serge Lancel's exemplary *Carthage*, published in 1992 in French, only goes as far as the destruction of the Punic city in 146 BCE. There are many articles on the Roman phase of the city in journals such as *L'Africa Romana* or the *Journal of Roman Archaeology*, but there has been no comprehensive overview of our current state of knowledge on Roman Carthage. The recently published *Companion to North Africa in Antiquity* (2022) reflects new perspectives and also a focus on the whole region of North Africa rather than just the city of Carthage in all the various periods of its ancient existence.[3] This is certainly the way forward – to look at Carthage as part of the wider landscape in the ancient Mediterranean and North Africa – but it does seems long overdue that someone should undertake an examination of the Roman city of ancient Carthage.

As might be expected, excavations that have taken place in the recent past often involve the re-examination of sites that were studied by the earlier travellers and archaeologists in the nineteenth and early twentieth centuries. A few of the many examples of this effort in the past decades include Susan T. Stevens' work at Bir el Knissia and the work by Colin Wells at the odeon.[4] In fact, it is the case that for most archaeological sites at Carthage, someone will have been there before and so reanalysis of old excavation material is constantly occurring. Recycling old material and applying new interpretations brings a much more nuanced approach to the results. The broader picture and integration of the landscape of whole sectors of the ancient city also allow for new urban approaches. For example, research into the way in which different monuments had an impact on the life of a neighbourhood in Carthage is exemplified by the excavations in the southwest quarter of the city from 2015 to 2017 by Rolf Bockman et al.[5]

It is not only by physical excavation on site that new knowledge is being acquired through investigating previous projects. Many scholars have re-examined materials alongside original reports to shed light on the archaeological history of specific monuments or locations. This is a rich vein of analysis, as the study of the origins of the lead in the curse tablets found at Carthage has shown. The reconsideration of sites such as the Cemetery of the Officials (by Jeremy J. Rossiter) or the Roman theatre (by Karen E. Ros) over the last few decades illustrate the ways that places can be re-evaluated.[6] How people lived and who lived in ancient Carthage over its long history are questions now being answered by the scientific revolution in archaeology. This new world has opened up through the application of DNA and stable isotope analysis of the human remains from old cemetery excavations. These studies help to establish a greater knowledge of the identity and individual stories of the people who were buried at Carthage, where they came from originally and what kind of lives they lived through dietary analysis. These kinds of studies continue to broaden our understanding of the place of Carthage and the ancient Carthaginians who lived there. As old theories are reconsidered and more evidence is brought to bear on traditional views, a new history of old Carthage is being written.[7]

The archaeological story of Carthage continues to evolve with new knowledge and perspectives. History can and is being changed by archaeological research there, while the scientific approaches to the ancient city and its varied populations over time are creating nuanced and different legacies that allow a much broader population to engage with this important world heritage. The loss, destruction and rediscovery of Carthage along with the progress made in archaeological technology and its application today have created a landscape where current populations and millennia of heritage co-exist. There is hope for a new future for ancient Carthage that celebrates and illuminates its many pasts.[8]

NOTES

Introduction

1 For Arab and Berber identity in this period, see Fromherz, 2018, and Maraoui Telmini, 2021 for interactions between indigenous North Africa, Carthaginian and Tunisian history and archaeology.

Chapter 1

1 López-Ruiz, 2021; Quinn, 2018.

2 See Kaufman, 2017; Pilkington, 2019.

3 Regarding the network of western Phoenicians, see Álvarez Martí-Aguilar, 2017; Doak and Lopez-Ruiz (eds), 2019.

4 For the extent of the Punic city, see Maraoui Telmini et al., 2014.

5 Melliti, 2016; on the city in the Punic Wars, see Miles, 2010; Hoyos 1998, 2005, 2007; Ortega, 2022. For the term Punic, see Prag, 2006.

6 See Ferjaoui (ed.), 2010.

7 Useful modern studies include Goldsworthy, 2003; Miles, 2010; Hoyos, 2003, 2007; MacDonald, 2015; Burgeon, 2015; Brett and Fentress, 1996.

8 Hurst and Stager, 1978.

9 On the Gracchan colony and the consecration of the land at Carthage, see Stevens, 1988.

10 Świerk, 2022; Bockmann, 2022.

11 Bockmann, 2022; Hurst, 2010.

12 Bockmann et al., 2018.

13 See relevant articles in Hitchner (ed.), 2022; Hoyos, 2021. Mattingly and Hitchner, 1995 is still relevant for context. For the urban cohort at Carthage, see Ricci, 2011.

14 For the Tophet excavations, see the full referencing in Chapter 7; also Hurst, 1999.

15 Dunbabin, 1978. For a contemporary account of the spectacles in his native Carthage, see Tertullian *de Spectaculis*.

16 Audollent, 1901: 321.

17 Musurillo, 1972.

18 For Cyprian, see Brent, 2012; on St Augustine, see Brown, 2013; Reid and Vessey (eds), 2012.

19 On the transition between classical to late antique North Africa, see Leone, 2013, 2007; Fenwick, 2013.

20 Wells and Wightman, 1980. On the Vandals, see Merrills and Miles, 2010; Modéran, 2014.

21 Miles, 2017: 391.

22 Bernt and Steinacher, 2008.

23 Bockmann, 2014.

24 Ma et al., 2021; von Rummel, 2018.

25 Details of this period are in Kaegi, 2010; Bockmann, 2019.

Chapter 2

1 Kaegi, 2010: 248–9.

2 See Fenwick, 2020, 2022.

3 For Kahina, see Kaegi, 2010: 249–53; Modéran, 2005; Fromherz, 2018. On the conquest narrative of al-Baladhuri (*Futūḥ*, 229), see Hitti, 2002.

4 Stevens and Conant, 2016; Vitelli, 1981.

5 Caron and Lavoie, 2003; Ladjimi Sebaï, 2003a

6 Early Islamic sources referred in Martinez, 2002; Sebag, 1998; Abun-Nasr, 2012; Anderson et al., 2018.

7 For the Arabic geographies, see Siraj, 1995. For el-Bekri, *Kitāb al-mamālik wa-al-masālik*, see volume with transl. by Mac Guckin de Slane, 1965.

8 King, 2021.

9 Fenna, 2002 for *empan*.

10 Greenhalgh, 2008, 2012.

11 Berti, 2003; Bruce, 2015.

12 Fierro, 2010.

13 Translation of al-Abdari's *Rihla al Maghribiyya* ('North African Journey') from Fromherz, 2021; see also King, 2021.

14 Fromherz, 2021; Valerian, 2021.

15 Devecka, 2020.

16 Fromherz, 2010.

17 For the tapestries, see Schmitz-von Ledebur, 2019.

18 Temime Blili et al., 2021. For the Ottoman navy, see Panzac, 1999, 2009.

19 Leo the African and Marmol published in English Harris, 1705.

20 Brotton, 1998.

21 Vitkus (ed.), 2001; Matar, 2005, 2009; Weiss, 2011; MacLean, 2004. See also Père Frere Pierre Dan, 1637.

22 MacDonald and Bingham, 2020

23 See Miller, 2009 and 2015 on Peiresc, including the annotated maps drawn by d'Arcos. See also Dakhlia, 2013; Tolbert, 2009.

24 Letters of Peiresc and D'Arcos at *Early Modern Letters Online*, Cultures of Knowledge, http://emlo.bodleian.ox.ac.uk. For the *Life of Periesc*, see Emelina, 1999.

25 Letters of Giovanni Pagni in Redi (ed.), 1829.

Chapter 3

1 De Chateaubriand, 1968 (1811), 402–9; Chaouch, 2018. Desfontaines' words as reported in Dureau de la Malle, 1835. Gibbon, 1776: vol. 7 note 26; see also Bacha, 2013.

2 Ford, 2015; MacDonald and Bingham, 2020; further references chapter 2, nn. 22 and 23.

3 Brahimi, 1978.

4 Boularès, 2011 for the beys of Tunis.

5 Edward Stanley, 1786.

6 Thomas Shaw's map was published in Shaw, 1738; Temple, 1835.

7 Giusti, 2018; Finely, 1990.

8 Boularès, 2011; diplomatic correspondence in Plantet, vol. 3, 1899.

9 Jean-Emile Humbert's collection is held in the National Museum of Antiquities in Leiden. See Debergh, 2000, 2000a; Halbertsma, 2008. For Dutch ex-prime minister Mark Rutte, see https://www.government.nl/documents/speeches/2016/12/05/short-speech-by-prime-minister-mark-rutte-at-the-opening-of-the-exhibition-the-art-of-the-islamic-book-from-leiden-collections-%E2%80%93-eastern-beauty-in-reproductions.

10 Halbertsma, 1995.

11 Caronni, 1805.

12 Debergh, 2000b on Borgia. For Chateaubriand, see n. 1 above.

13 Colley, 2003 on the Royal Navy in North Africa.

14 Halbertsma, 2003; Docter et al., 2015.

15 Falbe, 1833 and Dureau de la Malle, 1835; Falbe and Temple, 1838.

16 Falbe, 1833: 43.

17 Dureau de la Malle, 1835; Falbe and Temple, 1838.

18 See Chaouch, 2018 for the paradox of Carthage; Said, 1979: 171 on Chateaubriand.

19 Wright, 2014 (online resource).

20 Gran-Aymerich, 1998, 2001; Schlanger and Nordbladh (eds), 2008.

Chapter 4

1   *Illustrated London News*, Saturday, 12 March 1859.

2   Perkins, 2004; Abadi, 2013.

3   The most accessible work on Davis is Freed, 2011.

4   Davis, 1861: viii.

5   Davis, 1861: viii.

6   Audollent, 1901: 13–14.

7   Davis, 1861: 506.

8   Published in Rawnsley, 2014.

9   Davis, 1861: 533.

10 Davis, 1861: ix.

11 Franks, 1860: 208.

12 Freed, 2011: 15, 36–7.

13 Davis, 1861: 190.

14 Davis, 1861: 114.

15 Davis, 1861: 114.

16 Davis, 1861: 288.

17 Davis, 1861: 288.

18 Davis, 1861: 195–6.

19 Davis, 1861: 196.

20 *Daily News* (London), Wednesday, 5 October 1859.

21 Davis, 1861: 444.

22 Mendleson, 2003.

23 On the methods used for lifting mosaics, the most helpful is Freed, 2011: 83–92.

24 Dunbabin, 1978.

25 Davis, 1860: 225.

26 Freed, 2011: 180–1, 186–7.

27 On Beulé's career, see Billard and Chandezon, 2012. In their bibliography, they list twenty-two scholarly publications by Beulé. That he also had an important political career is less well known.

28 Beulé, 1861: 35.

29 Beulé, 1873: 44.

30 Franks, 1860: 236.

31 Davis, 1861: 187.

Chapter 5

1   On Flaubert and Carthage, see Green, 1982. Her fourth chapter, 'Salammbô and Nineteenth Century French Society', is insightful on the how the novel fits into the zeitgeist of the period.

2   See Chapter 3, note 15 for specific references.

3   Freed, 2011: 34.

4   Gautier's review was published in the *Gazette nationale ou le Moniteur universel* of 22 December 1862. Berlioz's review can be found in the *Journal de Débats* of 23 December 1862.

5   Jouvin, 1862: 1.

6   Published in the *Revue Contemporaine*, 31 December 1862.

7   On the rivalry between Flaubert and Fröhner (also known as Guillaum Froehner), see Strong, 1975.

8   On both men, the key text is Laporte, 2002. He includes a list of the younger Pricot de Sainte-Marie's publications as well as a table breaking down the find spots and final destinations of the stelae from Carthage.

9   On the significance of land survey, see Choi, 2017.

10 Pricot de Saint Marie, 1875, 1878.

11 Laporte, 2002: 223.

12 On Françoise Bourgade, see Gutron, 2008.

13 Gandolphe, 1951: 282.

14 Available online at BNF Gallica. The letters incorporated into the work provide a fascinating insight into the workings of the Academy in this period.

15 On the Serapeum, see Laporte and Bricault, 2020.

16 See Ennabli, 2020: 121–2 and for the general location on the Bordy map.

17 On the recovery of material from the *Magenta* in the 1990s, see Harrington, 1999.

18 Audollent, 1901: 20–1.

19 On the man and his mission, see Renault, 1994.

20 Quotation cited in Abadi, 2013: 325.

21 Conte and Sabatini, 2018.

22 Lavigerie, 1881. Several of his letters are discussed by Gandolphe, 1951.

Chapter 6

1   A full account of Delattre's work in Carthage is beyond the scope of this chapter. His publications are listed by Freed, 2001; see also Freed, 2008.

2   Bomgardner, 1989.

3   For background, see Heffernan, 2012.

4   De Villefosse, 1897: 694.

5   Audollent, 1904: 334–54.

6   See, for example, Frothingham, Jr., 1886.

7   On more recent excavations by teams from Bulgaria and Austria, see Dolenz, 2000.

8   Stevens, 1993. The second chapter discusses Delattre's excavations at the site (1922–3) and includes his unpublished notes, which are reproduced with transcriptions.

9   Bir Ftouha was re-excavated in the 1990s; see Stevens, 2005.

10 Bates, 1912: 141.

11 The Punic tombs found by Delattre have been published by Benichou-Safar, 1982.

12 Moore, 1905: v.

13 See Carlsen, 2020.

14 Published by Freed, 1996.

15 The archives of the White Fathers at Carthage have been digitized and Delattre's letters from that collection are available online: https://library.artstor.org/#/collection/87731690;browseType=undefined.

16 Freed, 2001: 4.

17 Most of the scholarship on the establishment of the museum on the Byrsa hill is in French, but for a contemporary view, see Stevens, 1906.

18 Lavigerie, 1881: 10–11.

19 Głuszek and Krueger, 2019. Of interest is that at the time of the gift, the Princess was being advised by Wilhelm Fröhner, who had been so critical of Flaubert's novel *Salammbô*.

20 For the history of the excavations of the theatre, see Ros, 1996.

21 On the productions of 1906 and 1907, see Sherman, 2021.

22 As detailed by Freed, 2021.

23 Freed, 2021: 246.

24 Freed, 2021: 239.

25 Freed, 2021: 251–2.

26 The Bordy map can be accessed via many websites, including that of the National Library of Australia: https://nla.gov.au/nla.obj-234525706/view.

Chapter 7

1   For background on the Destour party, see Seddon, 2009: 197–231.

2   Pedley, 2011. For a map illustrating the development area, see Kelsey, 1926: 22–4.

3   See Poinssot, 1928–9: 156–7 for the letter of intent. See Duval, 1969 on Poinssot; also Carton, 1913. Back issues of the journal *Revue Tunisienne*

(1903–21) include fifteen articles with updates and summaries on the work going on at Carthage.

4 Essential reading is Bénichou-Safar, 2004; Xella (ed.), 2013. See Ennabli, 2020: 265–83 for a full list of excavations. Xella (ed.), 2013 places the site in the wider Mediterranean world.

5 *Cabiria* on the White House lawn is mentioned in 'French Ambassador and Wife Soon to Take Ship for Visit to Paris Home', *Washington Post*, 27 June 1914; Gorzelany and Matusiak, 2016.

6 Bonnet, 2011; Quinn, 2011. Xella et al., 2013: 1199–207 in response to Schwartz et al., 2012.

7 Ennabli, 2020: 265–7.

8 For an account of the early discovery, see Saumagne, 1923 and Icard, 1923.

9 The article can be accessed via *Punch* magazine online: https://trove.nla.gov.au/newspaper/article/138698770.

10 Bonnet, 2011; Quinn, 2011; Orsigner, 2018.

11 The work of de Prorok can be read in both of his works: 1924 and 1926.

12 For details on de Prorok and his use of film, se Tarabulski, 1989 and 2004; Garciá Sánchez, 2014.

13 On Robert Alexander MacLean, see http://www.apaame.org/2014/12/research-robert-alexander-maclean.html.

14 The review of de Prorok's book is by Hayes, Jr., 1926.

15 Ennabli, 2020: 266–9.

16 For excellent summaries of the careers, along with key publications, see Ennabli, 2020: 28–9.

17 On the Eucharistic Congress and Carthage, see Coslett, 2017; Alexandropoulos, 2009.

18 An excellent resource for Bourghiba is available online: https://www.bourguiba.com/

19 See Willis, 2015 on Tunisia in the Second World War.

20 For the career of Picard, see Ennabli, 2020: 24–5; and on the mosaics in particular, see Ben Abed-Khader, 1999.

Chapter 8

1 For a recent appraisal of Tunisia from independence to today, see Chouikha and Gobe, 2015.

2 On the Picards, see Ennabli, 2020: 24–5. Colette Picard was also the author of one of the earliest modern guidebooks to Carthage, published in the 1950s.

3 Ennabli, 2020: 32.

4 El Kafi, 1970: 7.

5   An interesting overview on the UNESCO 'Save Carthage' project is provided by Humphrey, 1985. The article discusses the creation of the Roman and Paleochristian Museum at Carthage, paid for by volunteers from the non-profit organization Earthwatch along with the Institut National d'Archeologie et d'Art (INAA). After being closed for many years, the museum was reopened in late 2021.

6   Ennabli, 1992.

7   Lancel, 1992, 1995, 1999. All are available in English translations.

8   The UNESCO website has detailed information regarding the current state of the site and the history of its involvement at Carthage: https://whc.unesco.org/en/list/37. The World Heritage reports from 2011 to 2021 are available on their website: https://whc.unesco.org/en/soc/?action=list&id_site=37

9   See Kuznetsov, 2022.

10 See, for example, the article on the *Voice of America* website (3 September 2019), 'Battle of Carthage: Tunisia demolishes homes to protect ancient site', https://www.voanews.com/a/middle-east_battle-carthage-tunisia-demolishes-homes-protect-ancient-site/6175122.html; and, more recently, the article by Samia Hanachi, 'Illegal constructions at Carthage: who is at fault?', https://inkyfada.com/en/2021/09/03/illegal-constructions-carthage-responsability-tunisia/.

11 On the problems of accommodating the various demands of the site, see Altekamp and Khechen, 2013.

12 Megeirhi et al., 2020.

Chapter 9

1   Imed Ben Jerbania, as the director of Phoenician and Punic Sites and Monuments at the Institute National du Patrimonie in Tunis, conducted excavations at the Tophet from 2014. See Ben Jerbania et al., 2020. For another novel approach, see Pilkington, 2023.

2   See, for example, Docter, 2004; Miles, 2006; Miles and Greenslade, 2019.

3   Hitchner (ed.), 2022.

4   Wells, 1996. Stevens' work is discussed in Chapter 6.

5   Bockmann et al., 2020.

6   Rossiter's article is forthcoming. On Ros, see note 20 in Chapter 6. Recently on lead from curse tablets, see Skaggs, 2012.

7   For the potential in re-evaluating sites, see the use of the cemetery remains and stable isotope and DNA analysis in Ma et al., 2021.

8   For an excellent short discussion, see Khanoussi, 2015.

BIBLIOGRAPHY

Abadi, Jacob. *Tunisia since the Arab Conquest: The Saga of a Westernized Muslim State*. Reading: Ithaca Press, 2013.

Abun-Nasr, Jamil. *A History of the Maghrib in the Islamic Period*. Cambridge: Cambridge University Press, 2012.

Alexandropoulos, Jacques. 'Paul Gauckler (1866–1911): une évocation de son passage à Tunis d'après les fonds des archives départementales de l'Arièges'. *Pallas* 56 (2000): 119–37.

Alexandropoulos, Jacques. 'Entre archéologie, universalité et nationalismes: le trentième congrès eucharistique international de Carthage (1930)'. *Anabases* 9 (2009): 53–70.

Altekamp, Stefan and Mona Khechen. 'Third Carthage: Struggles and Contestations over Archaeological Space'. *Archaeologies: Journal of the World Archaeological Congress* 9, no. 3 (2013): 470–505.

Álvarez Martí-Aguilar, Manuel. 'The Network of Melqart: Tyre, Gadir, Carthage and the Founding God'. In *War, Warlords, and Interstate Relations in the Ancient Mediterranean*, edited by Toni Ñaco del Hoyo and Fernando López Sánchez, 113–50. Leiden: Brill, 2017.

Amadasi Guzzo, Maria and José Zamora López. 'The Epigraphy of the Tophet'. *Studi Epigrafici e Linguistici* 29–30 (2012–13): 159–92.

Anderson, Glair, Corisande Fenwick and Mariam Rosser-Owen (eds). *The Aghlabids and Their Neighbors*. Leiden: Brill, 2018.

Aounallah, Samir and Michèle Coltelloni Trannoy. 'De Byrsa a Carthage: naissance d'un topynome *Carthage*'. In *Carthage: maîtresse de la Méditerranée, capitale de l'Afrique (IXe siècle avant J.-C.–XIIIe siècle)*, edited by A. Aounallah and A. Mastino, 57–64. Tunis: Agence de Mise en Valeur du Patrimoine et de Promotion Culturelle Institut National du Patrimoine, 2018.

Aubet, Maria. *The Phoenicians and the West: Politics, Colonies and Trade*. Cambridge: Cambridge University Press, 1993.

Audollent, Auguste. *Carthage Romaine*. Paris: Ancienne Librairie Thorin et Fils, 1901.

Audollent, Auguste. *Defixionum Tabellae*. Paris: Fontemoing, 1904.

Bacha, Myriam. 'La constitution d'une notion patrimoniale en Tunisie, XIXe–XXe siècles: émergence et apport des disciplines de l'archéologie et de l'architecture'. In *Chantiers et défis de la recherché sur le Magreb contemporain*, edited by Pierre Robert Baduel, 158–78. Paris: Karthala, 2009.

Bacha, Myriam. 'Les écrits des amateurs européens: l'invention de stéréotypes'. In *Patrimoine et monuments en Tunisie 1881–1920*, 17–32. Rennes: Universitaires de Rennes, 2013.

Bacha, Myriam. 'Paul Gauckler, le père Delattre et l'archevêché de Carthage: collaboration scientifique et affrontements institutionnels'. In *Autours du fonds Poinssot: Lumières sur l'archéologie tunisienne, 1870–1980*, edited by Monique Dondin-Payre et al., 1–16. Paris: Publications de l'Institut National d'Histoire de l'Art, 2017.

Bates, William N. 'Archaeology in Africa, 1910'. *American Journal of Archaeology* 16, no. 1 (1912): 141–3.

Ben Abed-Khader, Aïcha et al. *Corpus des mosaïques de Tunisie IV. Karthago (Carthage) 1: Les mosaïques du parc archéologique des Thermes d'Antonin*. Tunis: Institut National du Patrimoine, 1999.

Bénichou-Safar, Hélène. *Les tombes puniques de Carthage: Topographie, structures, inscriptions et rites funéraires*. Paris: CNRS, 1982.

Bénichou-Safar, Hélène. *Le Tophet de Salammbô à Carthage: essai de reconstitution*. Rome: Collection de l'École Français de Rome 342, 2004.

Ben Jerbania, Imed et al. 'Nouvelles fouilles dans le sanctuaire de Ba'l Hamon à Carthage'. In *Un viaje entre el Oriente y el Occidente del Mediterráneo: IX Congresso Internacional de Estudios Fenicios y Púnicos*, edited by Sebastián Celestino Pérez and Esther Rodríguez González, 1141–56. Mérida: MYTRA, Monografías y Trabajos de Arqueología. Instituto de Arqueología 5, 2020.

Bernt, Guido and Roland Steinacher. 'Minting in Vandal North Africa: Coins of the Vandal Period in the Coin Cabinet of Vienna's Kunsthistorisches Museum'. *Early Medieval Europe* 16, no. 3 (2008): 252–98.

Berti, Graziella. 'Pisa città mediterranea: La testimonianza delle ceramiche importate ed esportate'. In *Pisa e il Mediterraneo: Uomini, merci, idee dagli Etruschi ai Medici*, edited by M. Tangheroni, 169–73. Pisa-Milano: Skira, 2003.

Beulé, Charles-Ernest. *Fouilles à Carthage aux frais et sous la direction de M. Beulé*. Paris: Imprimerie Impériale, 1861.

Beulé, Charles-Ernest. *Fouilles et découvertes résumées et discutées en vue de l'histoire de l'art. T. 2: Afrique et Asia*. Paris: Didier, 1873.

Billard, Yves and Christophe Chandezon. 'Ernest Beulé (1826–1874): Archéologie classique, histoire romaine et politique sous Napoléon III'. *Liame: Histoire et histoire de l'art des époques moderne et contemporaine de l'Europe méditerranéenne et de ses périphéries* 24 (2012): 1–28.

Bockmann, Ralf. 'The Non-Archaeology of Arianism – What Comparing Cases in Carthage, Haïdra and Ravenna Can Tell Us about "Arian" Churches'. In *Arianism: Roman Heresy and Barbarian Creed*, edited by G. Berndt and R. Steinacher, 201–18. London: Taylor and Francis, 2014.

Bockmann, Ralf. 'Late Byzantine and Early Islamic Carthage and the Transition of Power to Tunis and Kairouan'. In *Africa – Ifriqiya: Continuity and Change in North Africa from the Byzantine to the Early Islamic Age: Papers of a Conference Held in Rome, Museo nazionale Romano, Terme di Diocleziano, 28 February–2 March 2013*, edited by R. Bockmann, A. Leone and P. von Rummel, 77–89. Rome and Wiesbaden: Deutsches Archäologisches Institut, 2019.

Bockmann, Ralf. 'African Rome: The City of Carthage from its Roman (Re-) foundation to the End of the Byzantine period'. In *A Companion to North Africa in Antiquity*, edited by R. B. Hitchner, 117–41. Hoboken, NJ: John Wiley & Sons Inc., 2022.

Bockmann, Ralf, H. Ben Romdhane, F. Schön, I. Fumadó Ortega, M. Broisch, S. Cespa and H. Töpfer. 'The SW Quarter of Carthage and Its Main Monument: New Results on the Topographical Context, Construction and Development of the Circus, based on Fieldwork 2015–17'. In *For the Love of Carthage* (Journal of Roman Archaeology Supplementary Series, 109), edited by J. H. Humphrey, 50–74. Portsmouth, RI: Journal of Roman Archaeology, 2020.

Bockmann, Ralf, Hamden Ben Romdhane, Frerich Schön, Iván Fumadó Ortega, Stefano Cespa, Boutheina Maraoui Telmini, Yamen Sghaier et al. 'The Roman Circus and Southwestern City Quarter of Carthage: First Results of a New International Research Project'. *Libyan Studies* 49 (2018): 177–86.

Bomgardner, David L. 'The Carthage Amphitheater: A Reappraisal'. *American Journal of Archaeology* 93, no. 1 (1989): 85–103.

Bondì, Sandro, M. Botto, G. Garbati and I. Oggiano. *Fenici e cartaginesi: una civiltà mediterranea*. Rome: Istituto poligrafico e Zecca dello Stato, 2009.

Bonnet, Corinne. 'On Gods and Earth: the Tophet and the Construction of a New Identity in Punic Carthage'. In *Cultural Identity in the Ancient Mediterranean*, edited by E. S. Gruen, 373–87. Los Angeles: Getty Research Institute, 2011.

Bordy, Pierre. *Carte archéologique et topographique des ruines de Carthage dressé, d'après les relevés de M. l'adjoint du Génie Bordy, avec le concours de MM. le R.P. Delattre, le général Dolot*. Paris: Service Géographique de l'Armée, 1898.

Boularès, Habib. *Histoire de la Tunisie*. Paris: Cérès Éditions, 2011.

Brahimi, Denise. *Opinions et regards des Européens sur le Maghreb aux XVIIè et XVIIIè siècles*. Alger: Société Nationale d'Édition et de Diffusion, 1978.

Brent, Peter. *Cyprian and Roman Carthage*. Cambridge: Cambridge University Press, 2012.

Brett, Michael and Elizabeth Fentress. *The Berbers*. Oxford: Blackwell, 1996.

Briand-Ponsart, Claude. *Identités et cultures dans L'Algérie antique*. Mont-Saint-Agnan: Universités de Rouen and du Havre, 2005.

Brotton, Jerry. '"This Tunis, sir, was Carthage." Contesting Colonialism in *The Tempest*'. In *Post-Colonial Shakespeares*, edited by A. Loomba and M. Orkin, 23–42. London and New York: Routledge, 1998.

Brown, Peter. *Augustine of Hippo: A Biography*. Berkeley: University of California Press, 2013.

Bruce, Travis. 'Commercial Conflict Resolution across the Religious Divide in the Thirteenth-century Mediterranean'. *Mediterranean Historical Review* 30, no. 1 (2015): 19–38.

Burgeon, Christophe. *La troisième guerre punique et la destruction de Carthage*. Paris: L'Harmattan, 2015.

Burns, J. Patout and Robin M. Jensen. *Christianity in North Africa: The Development of Its Practices and Beliefs*. Grand Rapids, MI: Wm. B. Eerdmans Publ., 2014.

Carlsen, Jesper. 'Epitaphs and the Demography of the Imperial Slaves and Freedmen in Roman Carthage'. In *Reflections: Harbour City Deathscapes in Roman Italy and Beyond*, edited by Niels Bargfeldt and Jane Hjarl Petersen, 195–211. Rome: Edizioni Quasar di Severino Tognon srl, 2020.

Caron, Beaudoin and Carl Lavoie. 'Les recherches Canadiennes dans le quartier de la "Rotonde de L'Odéon' à Carthage"'. *L'Antiquité Tardive* 10 (2003): 249–61.

Caronni, Felice. *Ragguaglio del Viaggio Compendioso di un Dilettante Antiquario Sorpreso da Corsari, Condotto in Barberia e Felicemente Ripatriato*, reissued as

Ragguaglio de viaggio in Barberia, edited by Salvatore Bono. Milan: San Paolo Edizioni, 1993 (1805).

Carton, Louis. 'Le port marchand et le mur de la Carthage punique'. *Revue archéologique* 18 (1911): 229–55.

Carton, Louis. *Documents pour servir à l'étude des ports et de l'enceinte de la Carthage Punique*. Paris: Leroux, 1913.

Chaouch, Khalid. 'Chateaubriand's Time Travel in Tunis and Carthage'. *Nineteenth-Century French Studies* 46, no. 3/4 (2018): 254–69.

Choi, Sung. 'French Algeria: 1830–1962'. In *The Routledge Handbook of the History of Settler Colonialism*, edited by E. Cavanagh and L. Veracini, 201–14. London and New York: Routledge, 2017.

Chouikha, Larbi and Eric Gobe. *Histoire de la Tunisie depuis l'indépendance*. Paris: La Découverte, series 'Repères Sociologie', 2015.

Cintas, Pierre. *Manuel d'archéologie punique*, 2 vols. Paris: A. et J. Picard, 1970–6.

Colley, Linda. *Captives: Britain, Empire and the World 1600–1850*. London: Cape, 2003.

Conte, Giampaolo and Gaetano Sabatini. 'Debt and Imperialism in Pre-Protectorate Tunisia, 1867–1870: A Political and Economic Analysis'. *Journal of European Economic History* 1 (2018): 9–32.

Coslett, Daniel. 'Re-presenting Antiquity as Distinction: Pre-Arab Pasts in Tunis' Colonial, Postcolonial and Contemporary Built Environments'. PhD dissertation, 2017, https://digital.lib.washington.edu/researchworks/handle/1773/39969.

Dakhlia, Jocelyne. 'Une archéologie du même et de l'autre: Thomas-Osman d'Arcos dans la Méditerranée du XVIIᵉ siècle'. In *Les Musulmans dans l'histoire de l'Europe. Volume II: Passages et contacts en Méditerranée*, edited by Jocelyne Dakhlia and Wolfgang Kaiser, 61–163. Paris: Albin Michel, 2013.

Dan, Père Frere Pierre. *Histoire de Barbarie et de ses Corsaires, des royaumes et des villes d'Alger, de Tunis, de Salé et de Tripoly*. Paris: Pierre Rocolet, 1637.

Davis, Nathan. *Carthage and her Remains: being an Account of the Excavations and Researches on the Site of the Phoenician Metropolis in Africa, and other Adjacent Places*. London: R. Bentley, 1861; reprint London: Darf Publishers Ltd, 1985.

Debergh, Jacques. 'Voici les ports. Non. Jean Emile Humbert et la localisation des installations portuaires de Carthage'. *L'Africa Romana* 14 (2000): 469–80.

Debergh, Jacques. 'L'aurore de l'archéologie à Carthage au temps d'Hamouda Bey et de Mahmoud Bey (1782–1824): Frank, Humbert, Cãronni, Gierlew, Borgia'. In *L'Africa romana. Geografi, viaggiatori, militari nel Maghreb: alle origine dell'archeologia nel Nord Africa. Atti del XIII convenio di studio Djerba, 10–13 dicembre 1998*, edited by M. Khanoussi, P. Ruggeri and C. Vismara, 457–74. Rome: Carocci, 2000a.

Debergh, Jacques. 'L'esilio in Tunisia. Il fascino dell'antichità'. *Atti del Convegno Internazionale di Studi: Camillo Borgia (1773–1817)*. Velletri: 2000b, 45–71.

Debergh, Jacques. 'Voyageurs occidentaux à Carthage. À la charnière du XVIIIe et du XIXe siècle'. *Anabases: Traditions et Réceptions de l'Antiquité* 5 (2007): 236–9.

De Chateaubriand, François-René. *Itinéraire de Paris à Jérusalem*, introduction by J. Mourot. Paris: Garnier-Flammarion, 1968 (1811), 402–29.

Devecka, Martin. *Broken Cities: A Historical Sociology of Ruins*. Baltimore, MD: Johns Hopkins University Press, 2020.

De Villefosse, Antoine Héron. 'Rapport sur les fouilles exécutées dans l'amphithéâtre romain de Carthage pendant les années 1896 et 1897'. *Comptes rendus des séances de l'Académie des Inscriptions et Belles-Lettres* 41 (November–December, 1897): 694–6.

Doak, Brian and Carolina López-Ruiz (eds). *The Oxford Handbook of the Phoenician and Punic Mediterranean*. Oxford: Oxford University Press, 2019.

Docter, Roald. 'Carthage and its Hinterland'. In *Phönizisches und punisches Städtewsen* (Iberia Archaeologica 13), edited by S. Helas and D. Marzoli, 179–89. Mainz: P. von Zabern, 2009.

Docter, Roald, R. Boussoffara and P. ter Keurs. *Carthage: Fact and Myth*. Leiden: Sidestone Press, 2015.

Docter, Roald et al. 'Carthage Bir Massouda: Preliminary Report on the First Bilateral Excavations of Ghent University and the Institut National Du Patrimoine (2002–2003)'. *BABESCH. Bulletin Antieke Beschaving* 78 (2004): 43–70.

Docter, Roald et al. 'Radiocarbon Dates of Animal Bones in the Earliest Levels of Carthage'. In *Oriente e Occidente: Metodi e Discipline a Contronto: Riflessioni sulla Cronologia dell'Età del Ferro in Italia*, edited by G. Bartolini and F. Delpino, 557–75. Pisa and Rome: Istituti Editoriali e Poligrafici Internazionali, 2005.

Docter, Roald et al. 'Punic Carthage: Two Decades of Archaeological Investigations'. In *Las ciudades fenicio-púnicas en el Mediterráneo occidental*, edited by José Luis López Castro, 85–104. Almería: Centro de Estudios Fenicios y Púnicos, 2007

Dolenz, Heimo. 'Two Annex Buildings to the Basilica Damous-el-Karita in Carthage: A Summary of the Excavations in 1996 and 1997'. *Antiquités africaines* 26, no.1 (2000): 147–50.

Dunbabin, Katherine. *The Mosaics of Roman North Africa: Studies in Iconography and Patronage*. Oxford: Oxford University Press, 1978.

Dureau de la Malle, August. *Recherches sur la Topographie de Carthage*. Paris: F. Didot Frères, 1835.

Duval, Noel. 'Louis Poinssot (1879–1967)'. *Antiquités Africaines* 3 (1969): 7–10.

Effros, Bonnie. 'Reviving Carthage's Martyrs: Archaeology, Memory and Catholic Devotion in the French Protectorate of Tunisia'. *Archeologia Medievale* 46 (2019): 65–73.

El-Bekri, Abou Obeïd. *Description de l'Afrique septentrionale par Abou Obeïd el-Bekri*, translated by Mac Guckin de Slane. Paris: Librairie d'Amerique et d'Orient Adrien-Maisonneuve, 1965.

El-Edrisi. *Description de l'Afrique et de L'Espagne*, translated by R. Dozy and M. J. de Gueje. Leiden: Brill, 1866.

El Kafi, Jellal. 'Carthage Must Not Be Destroyed'. *UNESCO Courier* (December 1970): 4–8.

Emelina, Jean (ed.). *Peiresc: le 'Prince des Curieux' au temps du Baroque 1580–1637*, a translation of *Vie de l'illustre Nicolas-Claude Fabri de Peiresc* par Pierre Gassendi (1641). Paris: trad. R. Lassalle et A. Bresson, Belin, 1999.

Ennabli, Abdelmajid. *Carthage: 'Les travaux et les jours': Recherches et découvertes, 1831–2016*. Paris: CNRS Éditions, 2020.

Ennabli, Abdelmajid (ed.). *Pour sauver Carthage: Exploration et conservation de la cité punique, romaine et byzantine*. Paris: UNESCO/INAA, 1992.

Fagnan, Edmond. *Extraîts inédits relatifs au maghreb traduit de l'arabe et annoteés*. Algiers: Ancienne Maison Bastide-Jourdain, 1925.

Falbe, Christian. *Recherches sur l'emplacement de Carthage*. Paris: Imprimé par Autorisation du Roi à l'Imprimerie Royale, 1833.

Falbe, Christian and Grenville Temple. *Excursions dans l'Afrique Septentrionale*. Paris: Société établie pour l'Exploration de Carthage, 1838.

Fantar, M'hamed. *Carthage: Approche d'une civilisation*, I–II. Tunis: Les Éditions de la Méditerranée, 1993.

Fenna, Donald. *A Dictionary of Weights, Measures, and Units*. Oxford: Oxford University Press, 2002.

Fentress, Elizabeth and Raoul Docter. 'North Africa: Rural Settlement and Agricultural Production'. In *Rural Landscapes of the Punic World*, edited by P. van Dommelen and C. Gómez-Bellard, 101–28. London and Sheffield: Oakville: Equinox, 2008.

Fenwick, Corisande. 'From Africa to Ifrīqiya: Settlement and Society in Early Medieval North Africa (650–800)'. *Al-Masāq* 25, no. 1 (2013): 9–33.

Fenwick, Corisande. 'The Fate of the Classical Cities of North Africa in the Middle Ages'. In *Africa–Ifriqiya: Continuity and Change in North Africa from the Byzantine to the Early Islamic Age: Papers of a Conference Held in Rome, Museo nazionale Romano, Terme di Diocleziano, 28 February–2 March 2013*, edited by R. Bockmann, A. Leone and P. von Rummel, 137–55. Rome and Wiesbaden: Deutsches Archäologisches Institut, 2019.

Fenwick, Corisande. *Early Islamic North Africa: A New Perspective*. London: Bloomsbury, 2020.

Fenwick, Corisande. 'The Arab Conquests and the End of Ancient Africa?'. In *A Companion to North Africa in Antiquity*, edited by R. B. Hitchner, 424–38. Hoboken, NJ: John Wiley & Sons, Inc., 2022.

Ferjaoui, Ahmed (ed.). *Carthage et les autochtones de son empire du temps de Zama: Colloque international organisé à Siliana et Tunis due 10 au 13 mars 2004 par l'Institut National du Patrimoine et l'Association de Sauvegarde du site de Zama. Hommage à Mhamed Hassine Fantar*. Tunis: Institut National du Patrimoine, 2010.

Février, Paul. *Approches du Maghreb Romain*. Aix en Provence: Edisud, 1989.

Fierro, Maribel. 'The Almohads (524–668/1130–1269) and the Hafsids (627–932/1229–1526)'. In *The New Cambridge History of Islam, Volume 2: The Western Islamic World, Eleventh to Eighteenth Centuries*, edited by M. Fierro, 66–105. Cambridge: Cambridge University Press, 2010.

Finely, Gerald. 'Love and Duty: J. M. W. Turner and the Aeneas Legend'. *Zeitschrift für Kunstgeschichte* 53, no. 3 (1990): 376–90.

Ford, Caroline. 'The Inheritance of Empire and the Ruins of Rome in French Colonial Algeria'. *Past and Present* 226 (2015): 57–77.

Franks, Augustus Wollaston. 'On Recent Excavations at Carthage and the Antiquities Discovered there by the Rev. Nathan Davis'. *Archaeologia* 38 (1860): 202–36.

Freed, Joann 'Early Roman Amphoras in the Collection of the Museum of Carthage'. *Echoes du Monde Classique* 40, n.s. 15 (1996): 119–55.

Freed, Joann. 'Bibliography of Publications by Alfred-Louis Delattre (1850–1932)'. *CEDAC Carthage* 20 (March 2001): 1–59.

Freed, Joann. 'Le Père Alfred-Louise Delattre (1850–1932) et les fouilles archéologiques de Carthage'. *Histoire, monde et cultures religieuses* 4, no. 8 (2008): 67–100.

Freed, Joann. *Bringing Carthage Home: The Excavations of Nathan Davis, 1856–1859*. Vancouver: University of British Columbia Press, 2011.

Freed, Joann. 'Father Alfred Louis Delattre (1850–1932) versus Paul Gauckler (1866–1911): the Struggle to Control Archaeology at Carthage at the Turn of the Twentieth Century'. In *Life-Writing in the History of Archaeology*, edited by Clare Lewis and Gabriel Moshenska, 233–64. London: UCL Press, 2023.

Fromherz, Allen. *Ibn Khaldun: Life and Times*. Edinburgh: Edinburgh University Press, 2010.

Fromherz, Allen. 'The Making of the Maghrib: 600–1060 CE'. In *Oxford Research Encyclopedia of African History*, edited by Thomas T. Spear. Oxford: Oxford University Press; published online 28 March 2018.

Fromherz, Allen. 'The Saint and the Caliph'. *Journal of North African Studies* 26, no. 4 (2021): 642–53.

Frothingham, Jr., A. L. 'Review: *Archéologie Chrétienne de Carthage. Fouilles de la basilique de Damous-el-Karita* (1884) by R. P. Delattre'. *American Journal of Archaeology and the History of the Fine Arts* 3 (1886): 349–51.

Fumadó Ortega, Ivan. 'Colonial Representations and Carthaginian Archaeology'. *Oxford Journal of Archaeology* 32 (2013): 53–72.

Fumadó Ortega, Ivan. 'Punic Carthage'. In *A Companion to North Africa in Antiquity*, edited by R. B. Hitchner, 81–100. Hoboken, NJ: John Wiley & Sons, Inc., 2022.

Gandolphe, Pierre. 'Saint-Louis de Carthage: 1830–1950'. *Cahiers de Byrsa* 1 (1951): 269–307.

Garciá Sánchez, Jorge. 'Las excavaciones del conde Byron Khun de Prorok en Cartago (1920–1925): la colina de Juno y la difusión cinematográfica de la arqueología cartaginesa'. *Boletín del Seminario de Estudios de Arte y Arqueología* 80 (2014): 129–63.

Gibbon, Edward. *The History of the Decline and Fall of the Roman Empire*, edited by J. Bury. London: Methuen and Co., 1906 (1776), vol. 7.

Giusti, Elena. *Carthage in Virgil's* Aeneid: *Staging the Enemy Under Augustus*. Cambridge: Cambridge University Press, 2018.

Głuszek, Inga and Michał Krueger. 'Carthaginian Pottery in the Collection of Izabela Działyńska, née Czartoryska'. *Journal of the History of Collections* 31, no. 3 (2019): 174–5.

Goldsworthy, Adrian. *The Fall of Carthage*. London: Cassell, 2003.

Gorzelany, Dorota and P. Matusiak, 'Imaginary Carthage: From Giovanni Pastrone's "Cabiria" (1914) to "Game of Thrones" (2012)'. *Collectanea Philologica* 19 (2016): 117–28.

Gran-Aymerich, Ève. *Naissance de l'archéologie moderne 1798–1945*. Paris: CNRS Editions, 1998.

Gran-Aymerich, Ève. *Dictionnaire biographique d'archéologie, 1798–1945*. Paris: CNRS Editions, 2001.

Green, Anne. *Flaubert and the Historical Novel: Salammbô Reassessed*. Cambridge: Cambridge University Press, 1982.

Greenhalgh, Michael. *Marble Past, Monumental Present: Building with Antiquities in the Mediaeval Mediterranean*. Leiden: Brill, 2008.

Greenhalgh, Michael. *Constantinople to Córdoba: Dismantling Ancient Architecture in the East, North Africa and Islamic Spain*. Leiden: Brill, 2012.

Gutron, Clémentine. 'Mise en place d'une archéologie en Tunisie: le Musée Lavigerie de Saint-Louis de Carthage (1875–1932)'. *IBLA, Institut des Belles Lettres Arabes* 194 (2005): 169–80.

Gutron, Clémentine. 'Profils d'archéologues: la dialogue entre anciens et modernes'. In *L'archéologie en Tunisie (XIXe-XXe siècles): Jeux généalogiques sur l'Antiquité*, 110–14. Paris: Karthala, 2008.

Halbertsma, Ruurd. *Le solitaire des ruines – de archeologische reizen van Jean Emile Humbert (1771–1839) in dienst van het Koinkrijk der Nederlanden*. Leiden: Rijksmuseum van Oudheden, 1995.

Halbertsma, Ruurd. *Scholars, Travellers and Trade: The Pioneer Years of the National Museum of Antiquities in Leiden*. London: Routledge, 2003.

Halbertsma, Ruurd. 'From Distant Shores: Nineteenth Century Dutch Archaeology in European Perspective'. In *Archives, Ancestors and Practices: Archaeology in Light of Its History*, edited by Nathan Schlanger and Jarl Nordbladh, 21–35. Oxford and New York: Berghahn, 2008.

Hannoum, Abdelmajid. *The Invention of the Maghreb: Between Africa and the Middle East*. Cambridge: Cambridge University Press, 2021.

Harrington, Spencer. 'Sunken Frigate Yields Carthaginian Artifacts'. *Archaeology* 52, no. 4 (1999), http://www.archaeology.org/9907/newsbriefs/stelae.html.

Harris, John. *Collection of Voyages and Travels*. London: Thomas Bennet, 1705.

Hayes, Jr. William. 'Review of *Digging for Lost African Gods*'. *American Journal of Archaeology* 30, no. 2 (April–June 1926): 199.

Heffernan, Thomas J. *The Passion of Perpetua and Felicity*. Oxford: Oxford University Press, 2012.

Hitchner, R. B. (ed.). *A Companion to North Africa in Antiquity*. Hoboken, NJ: John Wiley & Sons, Inc., 2022.

Hitti, Philip. *The Origins of the Islamic State*. Piscataway, NJ: Gorgias Press, 2002 (1916).

Horden, Peregrine and Nicolas Purcell. *The Corrupting Sea: A Study of Mediterranean History*. Oxford: Oxford University Press, 2000.

Hoyos, Dexter. *Unplanned Wars: The Origins of the First and Second Punic Wars*. Berlin: Walter de Gruyter, 1998.

Hoyos, Dexter. *Hannibal's Dynasty: Power and Politics in the Western Mediterranean 247–183 BC*. Oxford: Routledge, 2005 (2003).

Hoyos, Dexter. *Truceless War: Carthage's Fight for Survival, 241–237 BC*. Leiden: Brill, 2007.

Hoyos, Dexter. *Carthage: A Biography*. London: Routledge, 2021.

Humphrey, J. H. 'A New Museum at Carthage'. *Archaeology* 38, no. 2 (March–April 1985): 28–33.

Humphrey, J. H. (ed.). *For the Love of Carthage* (Journal of Roman Archaeology Supplementary Series, 109). Portsmouth, RI: Journal of Roman Archaeology, 2020.

Hurst, Henry. *The Sanctuary of Tanit at Carthage in the Roman Period: A Re-interpretation*. Portsmouth, RI: Journal of Roman Archaeology, 1999.

Hurst, Henry. 'Understanding Carthage as a Roman Port'. In *Bolletino di Archeologia: International Congress of Classical Archaeology: Meetings Between Cultures in the Ancient Mediterranean. Proceedings of the*

17th International Congress, Rome 22–26 September 2008, Volume Speciale (2010), 49–68.

Hurst, Henry and Lawrence Stager. 'A Metropolitan Landscape: The Late Punic Port of Carthage'. *World Archaeology* 9, no. 3 (1978): 334–46.

Ibn Khaldoun. *Histoires des Berbères et des dynasties Musulmanes de l'Afrique Septentrionale*, 4 volumes, translated by de Slane, new edition published under the direction of Paul Casanova. Paris: Paul Geuthner, 1927.

Ibn Khaldoun. *Al-Muqaddima (Discours sur L'Histoire Universelle (Al-Muqaddima)*, French translation, preface and notes by Vincent Monteil. Beruit: Commission Internationale pour la Traduction des Chefs-d'Oeuvre, 1967.

Icard, François. 'Découverte de l'area du sanctuaire de Tanit'. *Revue Tunisienne* (1923): 1–11.

Ilahiane, Hsain. *Historical Dictionary of the Berbers (Imazighen)*, 2nd edition. Lanham, MD: Rowman & Littlefield Publishers, 2017.

Jouvin, B. 'M. Gustave Flaubert: Salammbo'. *Le Figaro*, 28 December 1862.

Kaegi, Walter. *Muslim Expansion and Byzantine Collapse in North Africa.* Cambridge: Cambridge University Press, 2010.

Kaufman, Brett. 'The Political Economy of Carthage: The Carthaginian Constitution as Reconstructed through Archaeology, Historical Texts, and Epigraphy'. In *Bridging Times and Spaces: Papers in Ancient Near Eastern, Mediterranean, and Armenian Studies, Festschrift in Honour of Gregory E. Areshian on the Occasion of His Sixty-Fifth Birthday*, edited by Pavel S. Avetisyan and Yervand H. Grekyan, 201–13. Oxford: Archaeopress, 2017.

Kelsey, Francis. *Excavations at Carthage, 1925. A Preliminary Report.* New York: MacMillan Publishing, 1926.

Khanoussi, Mustapha. 'Ancient Carthage in the 21st Century, A Timeless Message'. In *Carthage: Fact and Myth*, edited by R. Docter, R. Boussoffara and P. ter Keurs, 139–41. Leiden: Sidestone Press, 2015.

Khun de Prorok, Byron. 'Recent Researches on the Peninsula of Carthage'. *Geographical Journal* 63, no. 3 (March, 1924): 177–87.

Khun de Prorok, Byron. *Digging for Lost African Gods: The Record of Five Years Archaeological Excavation in North Africa.* New York and London: Putnam, 1926.

King, Matt. 'An Emir in the Ruins of Carthage: The Life and Times of Muhriz Ibn Ziyad (d. 1160 CE)'. *Journal of North African Studies* (2021): 230–57.

Krings, Veronique (ed.). *La civilisation phénicienne et punique: Manuel de recherche.* New York, Cologne and Leiden: Brill, 1995.

Kuznetsov, Vasily. 'The Jasmine Revolution in Tunisia and the Birth of the Arab Spring Uprisings'. In *Handbook of Revolutions in the 21st Century: Societies and Political Orders in Transition*, edited by J. A. Goldstone, L. Grinin and A. Korotayev, 625–49. Cham, Switzerland: Springer, 2022.

Ladjimi Sebaï, Leïla. 'Byrsa à l'époque punique: Identification d'un site'. In *Afrique du Nord antique et médiévale: Protohistoire, cités de l'Afrique du Nord, fouilles et prospections récentes, Actes du VIIIe Colloque international sur l'histoire et l'archéologie de l'Afrique du Nord. Tabarka 2000*, 125–38. Tunis: Institut National du Patrimoine, 2003.

Ladjimi Sebaï, Leïla. 'Byrsa au moyen-âge: de la "Basilique Sainte-Marie" des rois Vandales à la *Mu'allaqa* d'al Bakri'. *L'Antiquité Tardive* 10 (2003a): 263–7.

Lancel, Serge. 'La renaissance de la Carthage Punique. Réflexions sur quelques enseignements de la campagne international patronnée par l'UNESCO'.

Comptes Rendus/Académie des Inscriptions et Belles-Lettres 129, no. 4 (1985): 727–51.

Lancel, Serge. *Carthage*. Paris: éd. Fayard, 1992.

Lancel, Serge. *Hannibal*. Paris: éd. Fayard, 1995.

Lancel, Serge. *Saint Augustin*. Paris: éd. Fayard, 1999.

Laporte, Jean-Pierre. 'Les Pricot de Sainte-Marie, père et fils, et l'exploration géographique et archéologique de la Tunisie et de Carthage'. In *L'Afrique du nord antique et médiévale: mémoire, identité et imaginaire*, edited by C. Briand-Ponsart and Sylvie Crogiez, 207–74. Rouen: Université de Rouen, 2002.

Laporte, Jean-Pierre. 'Un archéologue en Tunisie, Louis Carton (1861–1924)'. *Bulletin Archéologique du Comité des Travaux Historiques et Scientifiques* 39 (2009): 239–64.

Laporte, Jean-Pierre and Laurent Bricault. *Le Serapeum de Carthage*. Bordeaux: Ausonius Éditions, 2020.

Lavigerie, Charles. *De l'utilité d'une mission archéologique permanente a Carthage: lettre a M. le Secrétaire perpétuel de L'Académie des Inscriptions et Belles-Lettres par l'Archevêque d'Alger*. Alger: Adolphe Jourdan, 1881.

Leone, Anna. *Changing Townscapes in North Africa from Late Antiquity to the Arab Conquest*. Bari: Edipuglia, 2007.

Leone, Anna. *The End of the Pagan City: Religion, Economy, and Urbanism in Late Antique North Africa*. Oxford: Oxford University Press, 2013.

López-Ruiz, Carolina. *Phoenicians and the Making of the Mediterranean*. Cambridge, MA: Harvard University Press, 2021.

Ma, Ying, R. Bockmann, S. Stevens et al. 'Isotopic Reconstruction of Diet at the Vandalic Period (ca. 5th–6th centuries AD) Theodosian Wall Cemetery at Carthage, Tunisia'. *International Journal of Osteoarchaeology* 31 (2021): 393–405.

MacDonald, Eve. *Hannibal: A Hellenistic Life*. New Haven, CT: Yale University Press, 2015.

MacDonald, Eve and Sandra Bingham. 'Piracy, Plunder and the Legacy of Archaeological Research in North Africa'. In *Piracy, Pillage and Plunder in Antiquity: Appropriation and the Ancient World*, edited by Richard Evans and Martine De Marre, 170–84. London: Routledge, 2020.

MacLean, Gerald. *The Rise of Oriental Travel: English Visitors to the Ottoman Empire 1580–1720*. London: Palgrave MacMillan, 2004.

Mahjoubi, Amar, Hédi Slim, Khaled Belkhodja and Abdelmajid Ennabli. *Histoire générale de al Tunisie, T. 1 L' Antiquité*. Tunis: Sud Éditions, 2003.

Maraoui Telmini, Boutheina. 'L'autochtonie à Carthage'. In *Être autochtone, devenir autochtone: définitions, représentations. Actes du premier colloque international de l'École Tunisienne d'Histoire et d'Anthropologie (25–27 octobre 2019)*, edited by N. Kallala and B. Yazidi, 61–8. Tunis: Centre des Arts, de la Culture et des Lettres 'Ksar Saïd', 2021.

Maraoui Telmini, Boutheina. 'La "Chapelle Cintas" vue de la ville à la lumière des fouilles préventives à Carthage'. *BYRSA* (Scritti sull'Antico Oriente Mediterraneo) 39–40 (2021a): 155–85.

Maraoui Telmini, Boutheina et al. 'Defining Punic Carthage'. In *The Punic Mediterranean: Identities and Identification from Phoenician Settlement to Roman Rule*, edited by J. Quinn and N. Vella, 113–47. Cambridge: Cambridge University Press, 2014.

Martinez, Ferdinando. 'De Carthage à Tunis'. In *L'Afrique du nord antique et médiévale: mémoire, identité et imaginaire*, edited by C. Criand-Ponsart and Sylvie Crogniez, 143–56. Rouen: Université de Rouen, 2002.

Matar, Nabil. *Britain and Barbary, 1589–1689*. Gainesville: University of Florida Press, 2005.

Matar, Nabil. *Europe Through Arab Eyes, 1578–1727*. New York: Columbia University Press, 2009.

Mattingly, David and R. Bruce Hitchner, 'Roman Africa: An Archaeological Review'. *Journal of Roman Studies* 85 (1995): 165–213.

McCarty, Matthew. 'French Archaeology and History in the Colonial Maghreb: Inheritance, Presence, and Absence'. In *Unmasking Ideology in Imperial and Colonial Archaeology: Vocabulary, Symbols, and Legacy, Ideas, Debates, and Perspectives*, Vol. 8, edited by B. Effros and G. Lai, 359–82. Los Angeles: Cotsen Institute of Archaeology Press, University of California, 2018.

Megeirhi, Huda A. et al. 'Employing a Value–Belief–Norm Framework to Gauge Carthage Residents' Intentions to Support Sustainable Cultural Heritage Tourism'. *Journal of Sustainable Tourism* 28, no. 9 (2020): 1351–70.

Melliti, Khaled. *Carthage, Histoire d'une métropole méditerranéenne*. Paris: Perrin, 2016.

Mendleson, Carole. *Catalogue of Punic Stelae in the British Museum*. London: Chameleon Press, 2003.

Merrills, Andrew and Richard Miles. *The Vandals*. Chichester: Wiley Blackwell, 2010.

Miles, Richard. 'British Excavations at Bir Messaouda, Carthage 2000–2004: the Byzantine Basilica'. *Babesch: Bulletin Antieke Beschaving* 81 (2006): 199–226.

Miles, Richard. *Carthage Must Be Destroyed*. London: Allen Lane, 2010.

Miles, Richard. 'Vandal North Africa and the Fourth Punic War'. *Classical Philology* 112, no. 3 (2017): 384–410.

Miles, Richard and Simon Greenslade. *The Bir Messaouda Basilica: Pilgrimage and the Transformation of an Urban Landscape in Sixth Century AD Carthage*. Barnsley: Oxbow Books, 2019.

Miller, Peter. 'Peiresc in Africa: Arm-chair Anthropology in the Early Seventeenth Century'. In *Les premiers siècles de la République européene des Lettres*, edited by M. Fumaroli, 493–525. Paris: Alain Baudry, 2009.

Miller, Peter. *Peiresc's Mediterranean World*. Cambridge, MA: Harvard University Press, 2015.

Modéran, Yves. 'De Mastiès à la Kâhina'. *Aouras* 3 (2005): 159–83.

Modéran, Yves. *Les Vandales et l'Empire Romain*, edited by Michel-Yves Perrin. Arles: Éditions Errance, 2014.

Montagne, Robert. *The Berbers: Their Social and Political Organization*. London: Routledge, 2019.

Moore, Mabel. *Carthage of the Phoenicians in the Light of Modern Excavation*. New York: E. P. Dutton & Co, 1905.

Musurillo, Herbert. *The Acts of the Christian Martyrs*. Oxford: Clarendon Press, 1972.

Orsinger, Adriano. 'The *Chappelle Cintas* Revisited and the Tophet of Carthage between Ancestors and New Identities'. *Babesch: Bulletin Antieke Beschaving* 93 (2018): 49–74.

Panzac, Daniel. *Les Corsaires barbaresques: la fin d'une épopée, 1800–1820*. Paris: CNRS, 1999.

Panzac, Daniel. *La Marine ottomane: de l'apogée à la chute de l'Empire (1572–1923)*. Paris: CNRS, 2009.

Pedley, John. *The Life and Work of Francis Willey Kelsey: Archaeology, Antiquity, and the Arts*. Ann Arbor: University of Michigan Press, 2011.

Perkins, Kenneth J. *A History of Modern Tunisia*. Cambridge: Cambridge University Press, 2004.

Pilkington, Nathan. *The Carthaginian Empire: 550–202 BCE*. Lanham, MD: Lexington Books, 2019.

Pilkington, Nathan. 'Forbidden to Sacrifice Humans or Eat Dogs: Revisiting the Tophet Debate though a Demographic Lens'. *Cartagine: Studi e Ricerche* (Rivista della Scuola Archeologica Italiana di Cartagine) 8 (2023), https://doi.org/10.13125/caster/5532.

Plantet, Eugène. *Correspondences des Beys de Tunis et des consuls de France avec la Cour*, Vol. 1, 1577–1700, Vol. 2, 1700–1770, Vol. 3, 1770–1830. Paris: F. Alcan, 1893, 1894, 1899.

Poinssot, Louis. 'Séance de la commission de L'Afrique du Nord'. *Bulletin Archéologique du Comité des Travaux Historiques et Scientifiques* (1928–9): 156–7.

Prag, Jonathan. '*Poenus plane est*. But who were the *Punickes*?'. *Papers of the British School at Rome* 74 (2006): 1–37.

Pricot de Saint Marie, Jean-Baptiste-Évariste-Charles. 'Bibliographie carthaginoise'. *Recueil de la Société Archéologique de Constantine* (*RSAC*) 17 (1875): 69–110.

Pricot de Saint Marie, Jean-Baptiste-Évariste-Charles. 'Recherches bibliographiques sur Carthage'. *Recueil de la Société Archéologique de Constantine* (*RSAC*) 19 (1878): 97–186.

Quinn, Josephine. 'The Cultures of the Tophet: Identification and Identity in the Phoenician Diaspora'. In *Cultural Identity in the Ancient Mediterranean*, edited by E. S. Gruen, 388–413. Los Angeles: Getty Research Institute, 2011.

Quinn, Josephine. *In Search of the Phoenicians*. Princeton, NJ: Princeton University Press, 2018.

Rakob, Friedrich. 'Zur Siedlungstopographie des punischen Karthagos'. *MDAI, Römische Abteilung* 94 (1987): 333–49.

Rakob, Friedrich. 'The Making of Augustan Carthage'. In *Romanization and the City: Creation, Transformations and Failures: Proceedings of a Conference to celebrate the 50th anniversary of the excavations at Cosa, 14–16 May, 1998*, edited by Elizabeth Fentress and Susan E. Alcock, 72–82. Portsmouth, RI: Journal of Roman Archaeology, 2000.

Rawnsley, W. F. (ed.). *The Life, Diaries and Correspondence of Jane Lady Franklin 1792–1875*. Cambridge: Cambridge University Press, 2014.

Redi, Francesco (ed.). *Lettere di Giovanni Pagni medico, ed archeologo pisano*. Firenze: Magheri, 1829.

Reid, Shelly and Mark Vessey (eds). *A Companion to St. Augustine*. Chichester: Wiley Blackwell, 2012.

Renault, François. *Cardinal Lavigerie: Churchman, Prophet and Missionary*. London: The Athlone Press, 1994.

Reynolds, Paul. 'From Vandal Africa to Arab Ifrīqiya: Tracing Ceramic and Economic Trends through the Fifth to the Eleventh Centuries'. In *North Africa under Byzantium and Early Islam*, edited by S. Stevens and J. Conant, 129–71. Washington, DC: Dumbarton Oaks Research Library and Collection, 2016.

Ribichini, Sergio. 'Autochtones et Phéniciens à l'aube de Carthage'. In *Être autochtone, devenir autochtone: définitions, représentations. Actes du premier colloque international de l'École Tunisienne d'Histoire et d'Anthropologie (25–27 octobre 2019)*, edited by N. Kallala and B. Yazidi, 293–306. Tunis: Centre des Arts, de la Culture et des Lettres 'Ksar Saïd', 2021.

Ricci, Cecilia. '*In Custodium Urbis*: Notes on the "Cohortes Urbanae" (1968–2010)'. *Historia: Zeitschrift Für Alte Geschichte* 60, no. 4 (2011): 484–508.

Ros, Karen. 'The Roman Theatre at Carthage'. *American Journal of Archaeology* 100, no. 3 (1996): 449–89.

Rossiter, Jeremy. 'In Ampitζatru Carthaginis: the Carthage Amphitheatre and its Uses'. *Journal of Roman Archaeology* 29 (2016): 239–58.

Said, Edward. *Orientalism*. New York: Vintage, 1979.

Saumagne, Charles. 'Notes sur les découvertes de Salammbô: 1: sur les sacrifices humains; 2: sur les monuments'. *Revue Tunisienne* (1923): 3–23.

Schlanger, Nathan and Jarl Nordbladh (eds). *Archives, Ancestors and Practices: Archaeology in Light of Its History*. Oxford and New York: Berghahn Books, 2008.

Schmitz-von Ledebur, Katja. 'Emperor Charles V Captures Tunis: A Unique Set of Tapestry Cartoons'. *Studia Bruxellae* 11, no. 1 (2019): 387–404.

Schwartz, Jeffrey, F. D. Houghton, L. Bondioli and R. Macchiarelli. 'Bones, Teeth, and Estimating Age of Perinates: Carthaginian Infant Sacrifice Revisited'. *Antiquity* 86, no. 333 (2012): 738–45.

Sebag, Paul. *Tunis: Histoire d'une ville*. Montreal and Paris: L'Harmattan, 1998.

Seddon, David. 'Dreams and Disappointments: Postcolonial Constructions of the Maghrib'. In *Beyond Colonialism and Nationalism in the Maghrib*, edited by A. A. Ahmida, 197–231. New York: Palgrave Macmillan, 2009.

Shaw, Brent. 'Lambs of God: An End of Human Sacrifice'. *Journal of Roman Archaeology* 29 (2016): 259–91.

Shaw, Thomas. *Travels or Observations Relating to Several Parts of Barbary and the Levant*. Oxford: printed at the Theatre, 1738.

Sherman, Daniel J. 'Staging Archaeology. Empire as Reality Effect at the 1906–07 fêtes de Carthage'. *Classical Receptions Journal* 13, no. 3 (2021): 336–67.

Siraj, Ahmed. *L'Image de la Tingitane, L'historiographie Arabe, Médiéval et L'Antiquité Nord-Africaine*. Rome: Collection de l'École Français de Rome 209, 1995.

Skaggs, Sheldon et al. 'Local Mining or Lead Importation in the Roman Province of Africa Proconsularis? Lead Isotope Analysis of Curse Tablets from Roman Carthage, Tunisia'. *Journal of Archaeological Science* 39, no. 4 (April 2012): 970–83.

Stanley, Edward. *Observations on the City of Tunis and the Adjacent Country with a View of Cape Carthage, Tunis Bay and the Goletta, Taken on the Spot*. London: printed by the author, 1786.

Steegmuller, Francis. *The Letters of Gustav Flaubert, 1857–1880*. Cambridge, MA: Harvard University Press, 1982.

Stevens, E. M. 'The Lavigerie Museum at Carthage'. In *Carthage and Tunis: The Old and New Gates of the Orient*, Vol. 1, edited by Douglas Sladen, 79–100. London: Hutchison, 1906.

Stevens, Susan. 'A Legend of the Destruction of Carthage'. *Classical Philology* 83, no. 1 (1988): 39–41.

Stevens. Susan. *Bir el Knissia at Carthage: A Rediscovered Cemetery Church*. Ann Arbor, MI: Kelsey Museum, 1993.

Stevens, Susan. *Bir Ftouha: A Pilgrimage Church Complex at Carthage.* Portsmouth, RI: Journal of Roman Archaeology Supplementary Series 59, 2005.

Stevens, Susan and J. Conant (eds). *North Africa under Byzantium and Early Islam.* Washington, DC: Dumbarton Oaks, 2016.

Strong, Isabelle. 'Flaubert's Controversy with Froehner: The Manuscript Tradition'. *Romance Notes* 16, no. 2 (1975): 283–99.

Świerk, Martyna. 'Roman Carthage – An Ethnic Conglomeration? A Study of the Anthroponymy of an African Metropolis'. *Antichthon* 56 (2022): 162–79.

Tarabulski, Michael. 'Recording the Past: Capturing the History of Archaeology on Videotape'. In *Tracing Archaeology's Past: The Historiography of Archaeology*, edited by A. L. Christenson, 179–86. Carbondale: Southern Illinois University Press, 1989.

Tarabulski, Michael. 'The Life and Death of Byron Khun de Prorok', in the reissue of de Prorok's *Digging for Lost African Gods*, 251–67. Santa Barbara, CA: Narrative Press, 2004.

Tedesco, Paolo. '"The Missing Factor": Economy and Labor in Late Roman North Africa (400–600 CE)'. *Journal of Late Antiquity* 11, no. 2 (2018): 396–431.

Temime Blili, Leïla et al. *The Regency of Tunis, 1535–1666: Genesis of an Ottoman Province in the Maghreb*. Cairo: American University in Cairo Press, 2021.

Temple, Sir Grenville. *Excursions in the Mediterranean: Algiers and Tunis*. London: Saunders and Otley, 1835.

Tolbert, Jane. 'Ambiguity and Conversion in the Correspondence of Nicolas-Claude Fabri de Peiresc and Thomas D'Arcos, 1630–1637'. *Journal of Early Modern History* 13 (2009): 1–24.

Underwood, Douglas. *(Re)using Ruins: Public Building in the Cities of the Late Antique West, A.D. 300–600*. Leiden: Brill, 2019.

Valerian, Dominique. 'Commercial Relations between the Hafsids and Christian Powers under the Reign of al-Mustansir'. *Journal of North African Studies* 26, no. 4 (2021): 654–64.

van Zeist, William, S. Bottema and M. van der Veen. *Diet and Vegetation at Ancient Carthage: The Archaeobotanical Evidence*. Groningen: Groningen Institute of Archaeology, 2001.

Vaux, William S. W. 'On the Recent Excavations at Carthage Conducted by Nathan Davis, Esq. and M. Beulé'. *Transactions of the Royal Society of Literature of the United Kingdom* 2, no. 7 (1863): 441–73.

Vitelli, Giovanna. *Islamic Carthage: The Archaeological, Historical and Ceramic Evidence*. Tunis: CEDAC, Dossier 2, 1981.

Vitkus, Daniel (ed.). *Piracy, Slavery and Redemption: Barbary Captivity Narrative from Early Modern England*. New York: Columbia University Press, 2001.

von Rummel, Philipp. 'Where Have All the Vandals Gone? Migration, Ansiedlung und Identität der Vandalen im Spiegel archäologischer Quellen aus Nordafrika'. In *Das Reich der Vandalen und seine (Vor)Geschichten*, edited by G. M. Berndt and R. Steinacher, 151–82. Vienna: Verlag der Österreichischen Akademie der Wissenschaften, 2018.

Weiss, Gillian. *Captive and Corsairs: France and Slavery in the Early Modern Mediterranean*. Stanford, CA: Stanford University Press, 2011.

Wells, Colin. 'Paul Gauckler et la colline de l'Odéon à Carthage'. *Ktema* 21 (1996): 157–79.

Wells, Colin and Edith Wightman. 'Canadian Excavations at Carthage, 1976 and 1978: the Theodosian Wall, Northern Sector'. *Journal of Field Archaeology* 7, no. 1 (1980): 43–63.

Willis, Mark. 'Not Liberation, but Destruction: War Damage in Tunisia in the Second World War, 1942–43'. *Journal of North African Studies* 20, no. 2 (2015): 187–203.

Wilson, Andrew. 'Water Supply in Ancient Carthage'. In *Carthage Papers: The Early Colony's Economy, Water Supply, a Private Bath, and the Mobilization of State Olive Oil*, JRA Supplement 28, edited by J. Peña, J. Rossiter, A. Wilson, C. Wells, M. Carroll, J. Freed and D. Godden, 65–102. Portsmouth, RI: Journal of Roman Archaeology, 1998.

Xella, Paolo (ed.). *The Tophet in the Phoenician Mediterranean*. Verona: Essedue Edizioni, 2013a.

Xella, Paolo et al. 'Phoenician Bones of Contention'. *Antiquity* 87 (2013): 1199–207.

Online resources

Lawrence Stager's 2014 Babesch lecture 'Rite of spring in the Carthaginian Tophet' is published online: http://www.babesch.org/downloads/BABESCH_Byvanck_Lecture_2014_Stager.pdf.

Jo Wright's 2014 post, 'Sir Thomas Reade: Knight, "Nincompoop" and Collector of Antiquities', is available online at the British Library: http://britishlibrary.typepad.co.uk/asian-and-african/2014/06/sir-thomas-reade-knight-nincumpoop-and-collector-of-antiquities.html.

INDEX